For Nora

Published in 2006 by SevenOaks,
An imprint of the Carlton Publishing Group
20 Mortimer Street
London W1T 3JW

ISBN 10: 1-86200-312-2
ISBN 13: 978-1-86200-312-5

Editorial Manager: Roland Hall
Senior Art Editor: Darren Jordan
Cover Design: Darren Jordan
Design: Ben Ruocco
Editing: Marion Thompson
Production: Claire Hayward
Cover photography: Karl Adamson
Illustrations: Andy Mckay, NAF illustrations
Typesetting: E-type, Liverpool

Printed and bound in Great Britain

10 9 8 7 6 5 4 3 2 1

Adrian Besley

SEVENOAKS

◎◎◎◎CONTENTS

Introduction   6

Chapter 1: We are the Boys...   8

Chapter 2: Bringing the Game into Disrepute   26

Chapter 3: It's a Funny Old Game   52

Chapter 4: Hosting Your Own Finals   66

Chapter 5: Germany!   80

What they say... What they mean • Glossary   124

INTRODUCTION

66 We always believe that in any circumstances we can beat England. For us, it is like something written in the sky. We feel we have so much more confidence when we play them, confidence that we will find a way to win – maybe on merit, maybe on luck. 99

Lothar Matthaus – before losing 1–0 to England in Euro 96

66 I'll be happy with a draw but if Germany surprise me I'll be happy. 99

Franz Beckenbauer before Germany's shock 5–1 defeat to England in 2001

66 I know that the fans in our country have one wish – to win the 2006 World Cup. That is also my aim... The potential to do that is there. We can do something, just like the Greeks did at the Euro 2004 tournament. 99

Jürgen Klinsmann after Germany's 0–2 defeat to Slovakia...

WHO DO YOU THINK YOU ARE KIDDING, MR KLINSMANN?

CHAPTER 1
WE ARE THE BOYS...

ENGLAND VS GERMANY

Nobody knows for sure why these two teams and their fans love to hate each other. Maybe it's because of the war, maybe because of the '66 World Cup Final, maybe it's because of Oliver Kahn, but whatever the reason it is nothing that can't be sorted out over a stein of bier...

... is it?

⦿⦿⦿ENGLAND VS GERMANY – A BRIEF HISTORY

We loathe their robot mentality, hate their diving, despise their cheating, are appalled by their arrogance and, most of all, resent their constant success. Equally passionate, the Germans express mixed feelings about the bagginess of our shorts. But where did this intense rivalry come from? Let's look at the history of an ever-smouldering feud...

1523
English merchants introduce football to Germany, whose national sport had previously been sausage whittling.

Christmas 1915
Private 'Nobby' Sidebottom nods home a hotly disputed injury time winner in the no man's land game between the trenches.

1938
Berlin. Infuriated by having to give the Nazi salute, Stanley Matthews' England dish out a 6–3 pasting and full-back 'Chopper' Bates cuffs Goebbels in a tunnel melee.

1942
Paris. Michael Caine captains a POW XI to a sensational victory over their Nazi captors – then the whole team escapes!

1966
World Champions! Bobby Moore, Geoff Hurst and an eagle-eyed Russian linesman ensure England assume their rightful place.

1970
West Germany win 3–2 but Sir Alf Ramsey's sense of fair play – taking his best player off to even up the sides – means England are the true winners.

1990
West Germany win on penalties, make Gazza cry and take their ball home. Bullies.

1996
England thwarted on penalties again after Gareth Southgate is distracted by a lucrative pizza advertising contract.

2000
At last! The end of 35 years of hurt as Alan Shearer gets England's long period of superiority underway.

2000
London. Seven months later. Defeat at Wembley ends Germany's painful period of inadequacy. England demolish the stadium in disgrace.

2002
St Sven's Day, Munich. England thrash their rivals 5–1, but astonishingly are not handed the World Cup there and then.

2005
The 'Football's Coming Home' hit – an age-old English folk song – is stolen by Jurgen and the Germans for their World Cup anthem. Beckham and the boys swear they will bring it back to its rightful owners.

○○○○ READ IT AND WEEP, JURGEN

BERLIN 1938
Germany 3–6 England

Over 110,000, including Goebbels, Hess and von Ribbentrop, crammed in to see their naturally superior Aryan outfit hammer the English mongrels. The English team seemed happy to perform a Nazi salute – though later Matthews said he hadn't wanted to upset that nice Mr Hitler, captain Hapgood was apparently just waving to a cousin in the top stand and Cliff Bastin was just asking permission to go to the toilet.

The game was part of Germany's 1938 World Cup preparations – their other strategy being to annex the whole of Europe and take their best players (a tactic modified by Jose Mourinho 65 years later). England had declined to enter, believing they'd only spoil it for everyone else by winning it so easily. In Berlin, they proved it, as Sir Stanley played a blinder and the rest of the team ran the Germans ragged. Man of the match went to the British Ambassador who offered Goering his binoculars every time England scored.

WEMBLEY 1954
England 3–0 West Germany

Germany had won the World Cup in Switzerland in 1954 beating the 'Magnificent Magyars', the legendary Hungary side. But even they knew they had needed a lot of luck, a dodgy Welsh linesman and the great Puskas still limping from the kicking he'd got in the 8–3 pasting Germany had received in the group stage.

Six months later, strutting along to Wembley, they soon got their come-uppance – victims of a virtuoso performance by the Clown Prince, Len Shackleton. The Gazza of his time – usually left out of England teams because 'they play at Wembley Stadium not the London Palladium' – ripped the p**s out of the World Champions. In what captain Billy Wright called 'a truly magnificent display of ball control, artistry, positional play – and sheer cheek', Shackleton ran the show, capping it with a memorable chip past the German keeper, Herkenrath.

Just to rub it in, England went to Berlin two years later and won by the same score – World Champions my arse!

WEMBLEY 1966
England 4–2 West Germany

The Germans really thought they could win this. At Wembley? Against Sir Alf's Wingless Wonders? With a Russian linesman? They'd cruised through the tournament with a mixture of brutal tackling, writhing around, getting players sent off – and some fine football, mainly by Beckenbauer and Seeler. Now they faced an uninspiring England side who'd left their best player – Jimmy Greaves – in the stands.

Within 13 minutes, thanks to Wilson virtually wrapping the ball with ribbons and a gift tag, Haller had put them ahead. But if they thought old England were done, they didn't reckon on Sir Alf's flawless grammar, the invigorating properties of a half-time English tea, Alan Ball irritating them with his constant squeaking, a seemingly endless supply of Charltons, Kenneth Wolstenholme's infuriating commentary – or the fact that, 20 years on, Europe, including the Swiss referee and the Russian linesman, hadn't forgotten being made to eat pumpernickel and sauerkraut for five years.

The country went mad; Nobby took his teeth out, Greavsie went on a 20-year bender, Martin Peters went home for cocoa and the Germans skulked home to work out how to make England fans' life a misery for the next 40 years.

2000 CHARLEROI, BELGIUM
England 1–0 Germany

It was a little like two bald men fighting over a comb. The once mighty Germans keeping faith with an ageing, unadventurous side full of carthorses; the seldom mighty England, under the guidance of Kevin 'I'm not cut out for this job' Keegan, scraping the national barrel with both Nevilles, Barmby, Wise and Keown. But let's not throw a wet blanket over a magnificent display of, well, football-of-a-sort and, more importantly, the end of 34 years of hurt.

The great tactician Kevin Keegan clearly out-thought the Germans with the cunning plan of getting Beckham and Gerrard to hoof the ball into the penalty area as many times as possible. That and his motivational techniques like saying 'imagine you are a great big giant who is really good at football'. Luckily such detail was unnecessary as German boss Voller seemed to think that veteran midfielder Lothar

Matthaus could keep Owen and Shearer in his pocket. Unfortunately, when Shearer pounced to head in the only goal of the game, 73-year-old Matthaus was still having a nap after his half-time bottle of Mackesons. Nothing else happened in the game – at all – but we celebrated like it was VE day all over again and the rest of Europe had a good laugh.

MUNICH 2001
Germany 1–5 England

It is always good to beat Germany. But in Munich. And a complete tonking! And – even better – it came as a complete surprise. England had come from an embarrassing friendly defeat against Holland and Germany were on course to win the group.

So nobody was surprised when Jancker put the Germans ahead on five minutes. It was going to be another miserable day for English football. But something happened to turn England into superheroes – Gerrard was unstoppable, Beckham unerring, Owen devastating, Gary Neville reached the heady heights of average and Heskey discovered where the goal was! And let's not forget the Germans. The self-proclaimed 'Best keeper in the World' looked like David James on a bad day, hatchet-man Novotny was hacking at thin air, 'gifted' midfield supremo Ballack was bollocks and bully of a striker Jancker was made to look like he was a shoe-in for a new cockney rhyming slang word.

With 15 minutes to go, Sven rubbed it in by sending on Hargreaves, a player the Munich club itself had nurtured. As streams of Germans left the stadium we were left to reflect that it was that easy. All that England had been missing for the past 30 years was a foreign manager with glasses.

CRY GOD FOR HARRY, ENGLAND AND ST GEORGE! ⊚⊚⊚⊚

Before England's quarter-final tie with Argentina in 1998, Tony Adams was rumoured to have spent the eve of the match reading Shakespeare's Henry V and in particular Henry's pre-match team-talk to his men before they went out to meet the French.

The World Cup Final of 1415 – naturally limited by the number of nations around at the time – saw England meet France at the Agincourt out-of-town stadium. The French were odds-on pre-match favourites, but the 10,000 strong visiting supporters (well-behaved apart from some burning of villages and the odd disembowelling) would witness one of England's greatest ever victories.

The French had a formidable record at the Agincourt ground, but the boss was not going to let his men be rolled over. In a pre-match team-talk vaguely similar to – if less poetic than – Graham Taylor's Euro '92 half-time talk against Sweden, King Henry told his stars, Bedford, Exeter, Warwick and Gloucester, that they could make themselves household names and reap massive merchandising earnings. A manager much in the Kevin Keegan mould, Henry was motivational, appealing to the men's ambitions rather than busying himself with tactical details. It did the trick. England waltzed through the French defences and murdered them.

Forget Wenger's silences, Mourinho's dossiers, Fergie's flying boots... this was the ultimate team talk:

> ...we in it shall be remembered;
> We few, we happy few, we band of brothers;
> For he today that sheds blood with me
> Shall be my brother; be he ne'er so vile[1]
> This day shall gentle his condition
> And gentlemen in England now a-bed[2]
> Shall think themselves accurs'd they were not here[3]
> And hold their manhood's cheap while any speaks
> That fought with us upon Saint Crispin's day.[4]
>
> *Henry V*, Act IV Scene III

[1] Probably referring to Lee Bowyer; [2] *Sky Sports Tapestry* had demanded a late night kick-off; [3] The great-great-great-great grandad of Gazza had bitterly moaned on being left out of the squad again; [4] Possibly in honour of Crispin le Rooney, who struck England's winner.

◐◐◐◐ CONFERENCE CALL COACH

While many complain about England having a foreign manager, Germany have a different problem: a German manager who lives abroad. Jurgen Klinsmann has a 6,000-mile commute to work from his home in Huntington Beach, California to downtown Berlin. His absence has led to critics calling him the 'Conference Call Coach'. The following is a translation of one such call between Klinsmann and his assistants.

Jurgen: Hello, Oliver. How's things in Berlin?

    Oliver (Bierhoff – German General Manager): Very cold, Jurgen, I'm at the Dortmund game watching Metseyer. It's pissing it down. How about you? Is it another glorious Californian day?

Jurgen: I'm just, er.. at the office...

Voice in background: Hey, Klinsmeister! Come on in, dude. Surf's up!

    Joachim (Coaching Assistant): Ballack is out of the Sweden game boss. Hamstring.

Jurgen: Scheisse!

    Joachim: It's not that bad. Only a twinge.

Jurgen: No. I've just fallen off my skateboard – I just can't do the half-pipe.

    Oliver: What about the Lehmann / Kahn decision, boss?

Jurgen: I'm starting to think maybe...

    Young female voice: Jurgy, the beach volleyball team need some more suncream rubbing on.

Jurgen: Er. I have another call on the line, guys. Probably Beckenbauer again. Talk later... Ciao.

ANGRY SVEN

England's World Cup qualifier defeat to Northern Ireland was their worst result and performance under Sven-Goran Eriksson. The normally mild-mannered Swede was said to have been incandescent in the dressing room after the match. Though none of the players would reveal what was said, a transcript of the confrontation has since emerged...

Sven: [knocking on door] Are you decent, boys? Is it OK to come in?

Lampard: No. Piss off.

Sven: OK. I'll see you on the bus.

Lampard: Only joking. The door's open.

Sven: [enters dressing room] Well. That really wasn't very good was it?

Becks: That's not fair. The lads did their best. Some of those Irish lads were a bit rough you know.

Sven: I'm sorry, David. But I just thought you all might have tried a bit harder. Obviously not you, David, or Michael or Frank or Stevie or...

Sol: It was the formation. It just didn't work.

Sven: The formation was fine. Becks was working on it all week. Now, unless you start playing a little better I'm going to have to make some serious changes.

Cole: What? Make Terry captain?

Rio: Bring in Shaun Wright-Phillips?

Rooney: Play three at the back?

Sven: I was thinking more like a new kit – with some yellow maybe. You lads need to look at your attitude – not you, David – a kick up the backside, try to pass a bit better, talk to each...

[players are heard making for showers]

Terry: Anyone got any shampoo I can borrow?

Owen: Close the door on the way out, Sven. It's freezing in here.

Sven: Er.. OK, boys. Well done – especially you David. [Sven exits room]

Stevie: Eh, boss, tha's a la round ahl way that's good like. Crouchy, he's called.

Becks: Good call – I'll put him in next time.

The manager's loyalty to his ageing players seemed to be going too far.

✪✪✪✪THOSE WE HAVE LOATHED...

Stefan Kuntz. Mainly for the name but also as he scored the equaliser against England in the Euro 96 semi-final and the whole country could be heard yelling his name.

Jens Jeremies. Ron Atkinson described him as a 'little ratter'. We had other names for this nasty piece of work. Had a crap goatee, turned his back on Munich 1860 for bitter rivals Bayern and once branded his German team-mates as 'pathetic'.

Andy Moller. For arrogantly strutting Jagger-style in front of the England fans at Wembley having scored the winning goal in the Euro 96 semi-final penalty shoot-out.

Oliver Kahn. A fine keeper, but arrogant, opinionated and mad as a piece of cheese. Called 'Genghis' after a kung-fu style attack on a player. His finest moment was his half-time talk against Portugal in Euro 2000: "We must win or we'll look like failures." The rest of the team laughed.

Bastian Schweinsteiger. Seems a decent enough chap, but doesn't his name translate as 'pig f**ker'?

Ulf Kirsten. Like Jose Mourinho, the East German (and later Germany) striker liked to keep dossiers. Ulf would pass his to the hated 'Stasi' secret police. One hundred caps, but you bet no one wanted to room with him.

Michael Ballack. His father has described him as 'uber-cool' (like the Eskimos and snow, Germans have 43 words for arrogant).

Lothar Matthaus. World Cup winner, World Footballer of the Year and most hated team-mate ever. Rudi Voller once advised him to direct his views at the toilet seat, Klinsmann told him to shut the f**k up and Stefan Effenberg dubbed him a 'cheeky big-mouth' and a 'quitter', for bottling out of taking a penalty in the 1990 World Cup.

Stefan Effenberg. The most talented player of his generation – better known for making obscene gestures at the German fans, insulting the nation's four million unemployed, shooting lights out in his hotel room with an air gun and shagging his team-mate's wife.

Harald 'Toni' Schumacher. One moment. His attempted decapitation of Batiston's head in the 1982 finals marks him down as the most hated goalkeeper in history (don't count Jens Lehmann out yet though).

THOSE WE HAVE LOVED...

Bert Trautman.

In 1949, 40,000 took to the streets to protest when ex-POW 'Traut the Kraut' joined Manchester City. His spectacular goalkeeping soon won them over, and when he broke his neck and continued playing in the 1956 Cup final he became the first foreigner ever to be named 'Footballer of the Year'. He was awarded the OBE in 2004.

And...

Jurgen Klinsmann.

The jury is still out. Is he the outrageous diver and play-actor whose plunge helped Germany to their 1990 World Cup triumph? Or is he the lovable self-effacing, Beetle-driving anglophile who charmed his way into Spurs' and then the nation's hearts?
All eyes on the Blonde Dive Bomber.

IF ONLY...

... Seaman had stayed on his line
... Beckham had been willing to risk his toe to tackle Rivaldo
... Becks had ignored Simone's tap
... Sol Campbell's goal had been given
... Seaman had stayed on his line
... David Batty had practised taking a penalty – just once
... Graham Taylor was never made England Manager
... Carlton Palmer was Patrick Vieira
... Seaman had stayed on his line
... They hadn't made Gazza cry
... Waddle had scored from the halfway line
... Waddle had hit the target from 18 yards
... 'Psycho' had kept his head
... Gary Lineker had bigger boots
... John Barnes had started the game
... Glenn Hoddle hadn't done a Glenn Miller
... Steve Hodge had brought Maradona down
... Shilton could have outjumped a midget
... Keegan and Brooking had been fit
... They'd built the side around Hoddle not Robson
... Don 'defend, defend, defend' Howe hadn't brainwashed Ron Greenwood
... Brian Clough had been made manager
... They'd picked Stan Bowles, Alan Hudson, Frank Worthington, Rodney Marsh, Charlie George etc.
... That Polish keeper hadn't had a blinder
... Bobby Moore had hung up his boots
... Gordon Banks hadn't got sick
... Sir Alf had kept Bobby Charlton on
... We'd had 11 Bobby Moores

We'd still be World Champions!

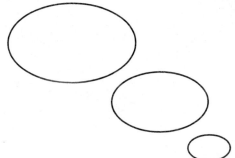

⊙⊙⊙⊙ENGLAND ONE CAP TEAM

The team who never got another game…

William Foulkes. At 22 stone, Billy 'Fatty' Foulkes was almost as mobile around the penalty area as David James.

Tommy Smith. When men were men and forwards were nervous, Tommy was a hero. Would break your legs before the national anthem was over.

Bill Nicholson. A gent, a great player and an even greater manager. He even scored in his only England game. Not bad for a full back.

Ian Storey-Moore. Without the Forest stopper, the double-barrelled name would be confined to England's 19th century roll call.

Neil Ruddock. Unfortunately, thanks to *I'm a Celebrity* and various panel games, 'Razor' hasn't been dispatched to the bottom of the 'forgotten' barrel.

Lee Hendrie. Irritating, limited ability, played for a Midlands club… Yep, of course, it was another inspirational Graham Taylor idea to give him a cap.

Andy Gray. No not the opinionated '70s Scottish goalscorer, but his namesake; an overweight, midfield makeweight. Did Taylor (again) play him just because he had a long throw?

Steve Perryman. Once promoted as England's great hope, Steve failed to get more caps due the wealth of other earnest, workaday carthorses clogging up the national team through the 80s.

Charlie George. "One cap?" I hear you say. 'Fraid so. The Arsenal and Derby lank-haired striker was too much of a rebel for Sir Alf and too much of a chirpy cockney for Don Revie.

Michael Ricketts. Having failed to shine in his allocated 45 minutes of a friendly, the Bolton hot-shot was unceremoniously dumped by Sven and never heard of again.

Alan Sunderland. White men might not be able to sing the blues, but Alan proved they could grow damn fine afros. No one can remember what he was like as a player though.

Subs: Nigel Spink, Michael Ball, Steve Guppy,
Brian Little, David Unsworth.

Manager: Peter Taylor...
So who's great idea was it to make Beckham captain?

CHAPTER 2
BRINGING THE GAME INTO DISREPUTE

HOME TIME! ⚽⚽⚽⚽⚽⚽⚽⚽⚽⚽⚽⚽⚽⚽⚽⚽⚽⚽⚽⚽⚽

They came, they saw, they went home again. Five magnificent, individual exits from the greatest stage on earth.

1. Roy Keane
Roy was a little unhappy at Ireland coach Mick McCarthy before the 2002 World Cup had even started. He went home, but not before launching a verbal attack on Mick. Link up these fruity phrases to make up your own version – it's bound to be close to the real thing:

> " crap player; off; crap manager; you; stick it up; your b*****ks; stick the World Cup; up your a**e; no respect; f*****g w*****r; ain't even Irish; you can feck; gobshite; you; this training ground's lovely; you. "

2. Maradona
Coming back from a suspension, USA 94 was to be his glorious swansong, but the manic way he celebrated his goal against Greece raised suspicions that he was on more than Lemsip. A positive test saw him sent home...

3. Zlatko Zahovic
He was Slovenia's most famous player and their only possible hope of making progress in 2002. When he was substituted in their second game, he turned on the manager, president and anyone else who'd listen.

4. Stefan Effenberg
Or as he would forever be known to German fans 'F'ing Steffenberg'. After a particularly poor game against South Korea in 1994, the blond-eyebrowed midfielder was substituted. As he left the pitch to boos from the travelling support, he replied by showing them his middle finger. Manager Bertie Vogts sent him home – saying he would never play for Germany again (he did though).

5. Willie Johnston
Willie was the first player ever to be sent home from the World Cup Finals for failing a drugs test. Quite how performance-enhancing the drugs were is unsure: the team suffered a 3–1 drubbing to World Cup minnows Peru.

2. Phil Neal (1982)
50 caps and yet, what is he remembered for? Being Graham Taylor's 'Yes boss!' stooge in the catastrophic 1994 failed qualification.

3. Steve Foster (1982)
The headband made 'Fozzy' look like a South American, his skills marked him down as the lower division clogger he was. However, he represented England in the 1–0 defeat of Kuwait.

4. Steve Hodge (1986)
Even when Bobby Robson changed the whole team round mid-tournament, Hodge survived – and let's not forget letting Maradona breeze past him like he wasn't there. He was there, wasn't he?

5. Terry Fenwick (1986)
England have had some great centre backs, Tel wasn't one of them. Every time he watches that Maradona goal, he, along with the rest of us, must think: "just trip him – now!"

1. Peter Bonetti (1970)
Replaced the great Gordon Banks in the quarter final against Germany in 1970, he let one in under the body and then was stranded in no man's land for a second.
Was he called 'the cat' because he liked to lick his balls?

ENGLAND'S WORST-EVER WORLD CUP TEAM

The honour of being handed the shirt with the Three Lions does something for your English footballer. Players of dodgy reputation, like Darren Anderton, Nicky Butt and Trevor Sinclair, have been inspired to play like gods. Thank heaven there are few that have let us down. But, lest we forget, here are 11 that have.

10. Steve Bull (1990)
Was a third division player when first capped by England. Did that not tell them something?

6. Robert Lee (1998)
The forgotten man of an unforgettable campaign. Best not to dwell on why.

9. Jeff Astle (1970)
Never really England class, Jeff proved it by missing an open goal against Brazil. Went on to become a milkman.

7. Graham Rix (1982)
Played every match in England's tedious finals – and no-one noticed!

11. Emile Heskey (2002)
What a goalshy England really needed was a striker who couldn't strike? What the left-sided problem really required was a player without a left foot? And, don't forget that annoying DJ goal celebration.

8. Ray Wilkins (1986)
Struggling against a poor Moroccan side, football expert and Mr Sideways pass, Ray chooses to throw the ball at the referee, get sent off, and nearly blow our chances. Talk us through that one again, 'Butch'.

●●●●NOT A PRAYER

In St Paul's Cathedral, an old England fan asks: "Oh Lord, when will England next win the World Cup?"

God replies: "In the next eight years."

"But I'll be dead by then..." says the man.

Meanwhile, in Notre Dame, a middle-aged French fan asks: "Oh Lord, when will France next win the World Cup?"

The Good Lord answers: "In the next 16 years."

"But I'll be dead by then..." says the man.

In Glasgow's Cathedral, a young Scotsman on his knees asks: "Oh Lord, when will Scotland win the World Cup?"

God answers: "Blimey, I'll be dead by then!"

"OK, one more time: when the ball is kicked
there has to be at least one defender..."

◗◗◑◑◑SCHADENFREUDE

That's German for "You thought you would win...
you were wrong, you were wrong."

1. Bulgaria 2–1 Germany 1994
Germany had reached the previous three finals and looked on their
way to a fourth when Matthaus gave them the lead with a penalty. The
Germans don't give games like this away do they? Not until the 75th
minute when Stoitchkov stroked in a free-kick and three minutes later
when the exquisitely bald Letchkov's diving header hit home.

2. Cameroon 1–0 Argentina 1990
Maradona and the cup holders strutted into the tournament's opening
game and walked into a brick wall. The Cameroonians proved not to
be 'naive Africans' but organised and, where necessary, ruthless in
defending their goal. Omam Biyak's header won the game, took the
Argies down a peg or two, but unfortunately didn't knock them out.

3. Senegal 1–0 France 2002
Even the Germans have never matched the arrogance with which
World Champions France arrived in Japan. Henry, Zidane, Vieira... they
thought they would walk their way to the final. But they were outplayed
by a team coached by a Frenchman (Vieira, as Roy Keane pointed out,
was Senegalese) and, what's better, went on to make a complete hash
of their other games.

4. Algeria 2–1 West Germany 1982
The European champions were favourites to win the cup. Coach Derwall
began the game saying "We're so strong we'll win without problems"
but 90 minutes and a lesson in creative football later was left claiming:
"I still can't believe this. It's beyond my understanding." Of course,
Germany made it to the final again.

5. Scotland 1–2 Brazil 1998
Half-time and John Collins' coolly taken penalty had given Scotland a
deserved equaliser. Did they really have a chance of beating Ronaldo,
Rivaldo et al? No. In the 76th minute Cafu struck a long shot from
distance, which Leighton dived to save, pushing the ball onto the chest of
oncoming defender Tommy Boyd and back to the net. Magnificently cruel.

PENALTIES

It's that time again. We all shake our heads: "What a way to decide a tie", "It's just a lottery really", "It's just so sad that someone has to miss". Some bright spark starts on "Can't they decide it on yellow cards or corners", others get really imaginative "Why don't they take away the tallest player from each team every two minutes". Meanwhile, everyone's really thinking: "Great, a bit of excitement at last – with the promising bonus of some arrogant twat crying at the end."

First you have to endure that interminable wait with loads of milling around. Finally, about half-an-hour after the final whistle, they emerge – a keeper leaping around like a maniac (who, after letting in all four easily, will be looking a little less chirpy for the final shot) and the first shooter, trying to look composed even though you know he's seconds away from soiling his tight-fitting lycra underwear.

High and wide, booming back off the bar, dollying into the keeper's arms... the result's the same – a consoling arm around your shoulder from a fellow player who really wants to throttle you or, even worse, a patronising hug from an opponent who is thanking God that it isn't him.

Blast it high: You imagine it rising into the top of the net, but end up with some twat in row Y waving it at you. As per Baggio in the 1990 World Cup Final.

Accurate: You think it's in, or at least you should be able to hit the rebound in, but slowly the truth dawns – you might as well have gift-wrapped it. Remember Matt Holland in Ireland's 2002 shoot-out with Spain?

Cocky, very cocky: You're a class player – not for you the fast bowler run-up or the aim for the corner and hope. Two steps and you chip it right down the centre. Except you look a prize gimp when the goalie stands there and catches it. Socrates did just that in the 1982 quarter final shoot-out against France.

Power: If the keeper gets anything on it, the ball will hopefully take part of him with it as it rips the back of the net. Either that or it will come back at you twice as fast. Psycho's powerdrive in 1990, for instance.

Oh S**t: You don't really want to be there. You might as well close your eyes like the rest of your team-mates. Now's when you wish you'd practised. Anyone reminded of David Batty in 1998 here?

THAT 1990 SEMI-FINAL PENALTY SHOOT-OUT AGAIN...

Shilton wins toss. England choose to take first penalty.

Lineker – SCORES – Keeper Illgner goes left, Lineker drills it hard and low to his right. 1–0. Looking good.

Brehme – SCORES – Shilts goes the right way – right, but Brehme's shot is unreachable, hitting the inside net. 1–1. He'll save one, we're OK.

Beardsley – SCORES – Great shot to the upper right side makes Illgner look ordinary as he grasps thin air. 2–1. It's our day, surely.

Matthaus – SCORES – but only just. Shilts diving to his right is inches away. Enough to make Matthaus chicken out of taking one in the final. 2–2. Lucky gits. But Shilts is on form.

Platt – SCORES – Illgner gets his fingers to it but just pushes the shot into the right side of his goal. 3–2. It's clear now, Illgner's not up to it.

Riedle – SCORES – Again Shilton chooses correctly, but flinging himself high to his left, the shot is too good. 3–3. OK. It was a good one – no harm done.

Pearce – SAVED – Hardly saved – it hits him. A great powerful shot that Illgner gets to just because he's too slow. 3–3. It's just luck. We're in trouble now.

Thon – SCORES – Low to the right. A younger Shilton would have turned it away. 3–4. It wasn't even a great penalty. We're still in it though.

Waddle – MISSES – A great long run-up followed by a skewed rising miss-hit. In cricket you get six and have a laugh. Here we got out. Bollocks.

"And some of the players can't watch..."

◎◎◎◎TEN WORST WORLD CUP REFEREEING DECISIONS

Brazil vs Sweden 1978 A decision so mind-bogglingly imaginative you couldn't make it up. Welsh referee Clive Thomas blows the whistle for full-time between a corner being taken and Brazil's Zico scoring directly from it with a header – after eight seconds of injury time. The man was a genius.

England vs Argentina 1998 "Looking back at the game now, the only thing I would change would be allowing Argentina to take the free kick very quickly after I had disallowed England's goal." Even after TV replays-galore, Danish poser Kim Milton Nielsen still manages to miss Sol Campbell's clear goal. Not just blind, but stubborn too.

England vs West Germany 1990 Ramiz Wright of Brazil fell hook, line and sinker when Thomas Berthold crumpled under Gazza's tackle. The booking would keep Gascoigne out of the final but, of course, we wouldn't get there because the Geordie boy's tears destroyed the whole equilibrium of the team.

Spain vs South Korea 2002 Two howlers for the price of one game. Firstly, Egyptian referee Gamal Ghandour disallows Helguera's opener for some non-existent 'pushing', then as Morientes heads home Joaquin's cross to score Spain's golden goal winner, the referee's assistant, Michael Ragoonath (Trinidad and Tobago), incredibly rules out the goal after he decides the ball had gone out of play before the cross.

South Korea vs Italy 2002 Damiano Tommasi latches on to a superbly-angled through-ball and slips the ball home for a golden goal winner. Ref Byron Moreno, however, sees it differently and gives the most ridiculous offside decision. Only months later, the same ref earned a 20-match suspension when he added more than ten minutes of injury time to an Ecuadorian League game. Liga de Quito scored in the 99th and 101st minutes to come from behind and win 4–3. At the time, Moreno was running for a city council position in Quito.

England vs Argentina 1986 Shilton, six-foot-plenty, loses out on a high ball to Maradona, five-foot-not-much, and ref Ali Bennaceur doesn't suspect foul play. It was the Tunisian's first and last World Cup game as a referee.

Belgium vs Brazil 1994 Even Belgium have their hard luck stories. They could easily have put eventual champions Brazil out of the finals if Jamaican ref Peter Predeghast had not, completely illogically, disallowed Wilmots' superb header. At least he had the decency to apologise at half-time – are you listening, Kim Milton Nielsen?

England vs West Germany 1966 It was the decision that turned a World Cup Final. With England 2-1 up and only 12 minutes to go, Swiss referee Gottfried Dienst awards the Germans a nonsensical free-kick when Held backs into Charlton. Then he completely misses a blatant handball by Schnellinger before Weber slams home an equaliser, forcing the match into extra time. Strange, as the ref had a perfect game otherwise.

France vs Kuwait 1982 With only minutes remaining in their 1982 match, France looked to have gone 4-1 up with a sweetly taken goal by Giresse. The Kuwaiti players protested that they'd stopped playing because they'd heard a whistle blown by somebody in the crowd, and not the fittingly-named referee Miroslav Stupar. Up in the stands, Kuwait's prince, Sheikh Fahad Al-Ahmad Al-Jaber Al-Sabah, stood up and waved his players off the field. The sheikh marched down to the field in his billowing pink robes and commanded the referee to nullify the goal. And without argument, the official obeyed.

England vs USA 1950 England were the laughing stock of the world after the USA's astounding 1-0 victory, but history has erased the part played by the wonderfully named Italian referee Generoso Dattilo. Shots from Mortenson and Ramsey both crossed the line but weren't given, and Mortenson was clean through when rugby-tackled by Colombo – no penalty, no justice.

WORLD (CUP) WAR ⊛⊛⊛⊛⊛⊛⊛⊛⊛⊛⊛⊛⊛⊛⊛⊛⊛⊛⊛⊛⊛⊛

Never the greatest of friends – neighbours El Salvador and Honduras met in a 1969 World Cup qualifying match during a tense political period and all hell broke lose. After having rotten eggs and dead rats flung at them, the Hondurans beat a retreat from the stadium in armoured cars and were flown home to safety.

❝ We're awfully lucky that we lost, ❞
said Honduras' coach, Mario Griffin.

Instead the Salvadorans took it out on the visiting Honduran fans, setting over 100 of their cars on fire. If you think it's bloody awful driving back up or down the M1 after a defeat, imagine how they felt trying to flee for the border on foot, but being constantly ambushed along the way. Next, the Salvadoran government joined in, dropping a bomb on the Honduran capital, then sending troops across the border. The conflict lasted 100 hours and left an estimated 6,000 dead.

⦾⦿⦿⦿HOW IMPORTANT IS THE WORLD CUP?

Ask someone who'd know: Ronaldo, Brazil's guinea-pig-faced goal machine. Shortly after the game, the scorer of two goals in the 2002 final – still on a well-publicised sex fast – was asked: "What is more rewarding – winning the World Cup or having sex after going without it for 40 days?"

The overbiter gathered his composure and answered in a way designed to please his coach, Felipe Scolari.

> ❝ Winning the World Cup is more rewarding, **he insisted.** I will have sex in a few moments, but the World Cup only happens every four years. ❞

As he left the press conference, 40 pairs of straining eyes followed the striker out of the door...

⦾⦿⦿⦿OH! DA COLOGNE

Spanish goalie Santiago Canizares was showering in his hotel on the eve of the team's departure for Korea when he tried to catch a falling bottle of cologne with his foot. The bottle smashed, slicing through tendons in his big toe. He missed the tournament.

⚽⚽⚽ MAMA MIA – HERE WE GO AGAIN...

As every Italian is taught at their mother's knee, Italy is the best footballing nation in the world – no-one can touch the great *Azzuri* players like Maldini, Riva, Rossi and some others. They have the best managers and the most stylish kit. It is truly baffling why they don't win every tournament. Now the Polytechnic of North Rome has scientifically researched every game and has come up with the answer: It's Not Fair.

- Other teams' players are jealous of their tans and good looks.
- Italian players are very sensitively nurtured and can fall down through a strong gust of wind.
- Draws always land Italy with 'difficult' teams – often whole countries.
- Players like Del Piero don't want to risk expensive haircuts against lesser countries like Spain.
- Other cultures – South Americans, Asians, Northern Europeans, Greeks, Swiss – don't understand the complex sensibilities of the Italian gamesmanship (often known as cheating).
- Neighbouring countries (like Sweden and Denmark), no matter how much they hate each other and how illogical it is, will conspire to eliminate an Italian team.
- It hasn't been fully explained to developing footballing nations that Italy have always been good at football.
- Foreigners playing in Serie A are ungrateful and often play well or even score against the hand that feeds them.
- Foreign referees are not up to the standards set in Serie A. Some have even been known to refuse bribes and ignore intimidation.

And there's you thinking it was because they weren't good enough to defend 1–0 leads, get caught out for cheating and played a carthorse named Vieri up front who couldn't hit a big barn door with a US Air force precision missile.

Coach made sure the Italians were well-briefed for the after-game interviews.

◉◉◉◉ANIMALS! THE TEN MOST X-RATED CHALLENGES IN WORLD CUP HISTORY

1. 1990 Cameroon v Argentina
Benjamin Massing on Claudio Caniggia

Benny took the credit – applauding his own heroics as he left the field – but it was more of a tag team effort. Baulked in his own half, the irritating Caniggia ran on; barely avoiding an agricultural hack, he body swerved away only to be met with the full force of Massing's hulking body check. Painful.

2. 2002 Mexico v USA
Rafael Marquez on Cobi Jones

With his side 2–0 down, the Mexican captain was sent off for a mid-air torpedo on Cobi that would have won perfect sixes from the judges. His simultaneous head butt and kick-to-the-ribs-kung-fu-manoeuvre had grace and power. But, just in case, as Marquez got his marching orders, two team-mates were busy stamping on the effete American striker.

3. 1966 England v France
Nobby Stiles on Jacques Simon

When the Frenchman went down in a heap and never got up, the world realised England were serious about winning the ultimate prize. The gruesome slide tackle looked horrific enough for the FA to demand Stiles be dropped. Sir Alf called their bluff, while Nobby blamed it on his bad eyesight.

4. 1962 Italy v Chile
Mario David on Leonel Sanchez

"The game you're about to see is the most stupid, appalling, disgusting and disgraceful exhibition of football possibly in the history of the game," said David Coleman. In a match full of spitting, punching and kicking, where Maschio had his nose broken, David topped them all with a karate-kick to Sanchez's neck. They just don't have matches like this anymore.

5. 1982 Argentina v Brazil
Diego Maradona on Joao Batista

Little Diego wasn't impressing in his first World Cup. He'd been kicked out of the Italy match and marked out of the Brazil game. He did what any of the greats of football history would do: waited until the last couple of minutes and kicked his marker right in the knackers. Classy.

By the second half, the referee was
struggling to retain control.

6. 1994 Brazil v USA
Leonardo on Tab Ramos

The world could see that it was GBH on a grand scale – except for Kevin
Keegan. The ITV panellist was adamant, even watching the slo-mos
saying "I didn't think he had done that much wrong". Maybe not, Kev.
Leonardo's elbow only fractured Ramos' skull!

7. 1986 Scotland v Uruguay
Jose Batista on Gordon Strachan

Scotland needed to win to qualify, Uruguay needed just a draw.
Batista knew just what he was doing when he went through Strachan
– Scotland's only decent player – and out the other side after just 55
seconds. Still, even against ten men Scotland failed to score.

8. 1974 Holland v Brazil
Luis Pereira on Johan Neeskens

Cruyff and Neeskens were running the show. Neeskens had already been
knocked cold by Peres, but he'd got up again and tormented them some
more. So, with five minutes left, Pereira went in waist-high, studs first,
and as late as the second post.

9. 2002 Portugal v South Korea
Joao Pinto on Park Ji-Sung

When the Portuguese midfielder clattered into the back of the skilful
Korean, sanctimonious journalists muttered to each other about it being
the worst foul of the tournament. But better still was Pinto's body punch
into the ample gut of referee Angel Sanchez. He got a four-month ban,
but thanks, Joao, we've all been there.

10. 1982 West Germany v France
Harald Schumacher on Patrick Battiston

The German goalkeeper smashed his arm into the Frenchman's face
knocking him cold and damn near killing him. Well there's nothing
clever about that. Except he got away scot-free and won a goal kick. You
have to hand it to the Germans.

CONSPIRACY!

Hardly a World Cup goes by without someone yelling 'Fix'. Nothing's ever been proved, but here are the charges and the verdicts...

1962 Chile – Italy vs Chile

In front of nearly 70,000 spectators in Santiago, Italy faced hosts Chile. Italian journalists had done their bit to wind the Chileans up and when Italy's Giorgio Ferrini was sent off in the 12th minute after a cynical foul, the South Americans went beserk. Leonel Sanchez broke Italian captain Maschio's nose with a left hook, but the ref let him stay on the pitch and dismissed Italian Mario David for retaliating and kicking Sanchez. Police had to intervene three times before Chile eventually won the match 2–0.

Conspiracy Theory: With the tacit agreement of the English referee, the Chileans kicked the Italians off the park throughout the whole game, but the ref sent off two totally innocent Italian players, thus handing the game to the hosts.

Verdict: Not proved. Referee Ken Aston admittedly had a stinker, but hey! Why would Chile have bothered? They were much the better of the Italian side, which was also easily beaten by the USSR.

1966 England – England vs Argentina and West Germany vs Uruguay

Both quarter-final matches saw the top European and South American teams meet each other. In bad-tempered games, both saw South American players sent off and England and West Germany progress to the semi-finals.

Conspiracy Theory: South Americans have long been bitter about this one. They point to the fact that FIFA assigned a German referee to the England game, and an English referee to the West Germany game. Also, World Champions Brazil, who went out at the group stage, had every match refereed by Englishmen who conveniently turned a blind eye to the assault and battery on Pele. England played all their games at Wembley and, of course, benefited from *that* decision.

Verdict: Ridiculous. Ramsey's wingless wonders didn't need the German's help. And as for Hurst's goal – *it didn't matter* – we got another one!

1970 Mexico – England vs West Germany

With England 2–0 up and strolling to victory, some suspect goalkeeping by stand-in keeper Peter Bonetti – unwittingly – allowed the Germans back into the game and eventually to score the winning goal.

Conspiracy Theory: Having failed with their attempt to get Bobby Moore incarcerated for stealing a bracelet, the South Americans, Mexicans, the KGB, CIA, BHS or someone put something dodgy in Gordon Banks' *cerveza*. The next day he faced Montezuma's revenge, while England were left with Bonetti's balls-ups.

Verdict: Hmmm! Compelling evidence. It's not as if Sir Alf took England's best player off or anything – whoops!

1978 Argentina – Argentina vs Peru

Argentina, the hosts, kicked off knowing what they had to do to make the final: win by three goals while scoring at least four. They won 6-0: knocking the unbeaten Brazil out in the process.

Conspiracy Theory: Brazilians, and the rest of the world, believe Peru threw the game. The result was all too convenient. Peru fielded four inexperienced reserves and a goalkeeper who was born in Argentina – and they received 35,000 tons of Argentine grain as a 'humanitarian' gift shortly after the game.

Verdict: Unlikely. Peru were already going to finish bottom of the group and had nothing to play for. They had progressed this far only managing to score against Iran and Scotland, while Argentina were a team on the rise, with a nation behind them. Peru even managed to hit the post early on and the 'Argentinian' made some great saves.

1982 Spain – West Germany vs Austria

For both to progress in the tournament – at the expense of surprise package Algeria – West Germany had to win and Austria had to lose by less than two goals. Somehow, the two sides, speaking the same language, managed to do just that. After a simple West German goal on 11 minutes, the two sides played a love-in, all tackling about as hard as Glenn Hoddle when he was very annoyed.

Conspiracy Theory: We suggest, ladies and gentleman of the jury, that the two European sides did conspire in mutual interest to end the participation of the North African side, who had already marvellously humiliated the Germans.

Verdict: Guilty as charged. A shameless arrangement that enabled West Germany to make yet another final.

2002 South Korea – South Korea vs Spain and Italy

Through a series of dubious refereeing decisions the South Koreans, a talented but hardly world-beating team, won their way through to the semi-finals; eliminating tournament favourites Spain and Italy on the way.

Conspiracy Theory: Both Italy and Spain threw massive tantrums blaming just about everyone: FIFA rigged the tournament to increase soccer's popularity in the lucrative Asian market; referees were in the pay of Far East gambling rackets or it was all a plot to get rid of Italy.

Verdict: Get over it! We all get a few dodgy results – look to Vieri, who missed a sitter for Italy in extra time, or Totti, who might have scored if he didn't spend so much time flinging himself to the ground.

◑◑◑ MR O.G.

A simple twist of fate and courtesy of the shin, ear or backside of your clumsy oaf of a defender, you're heading back to the hotel to pack your bags.

1. Berti Vogts 1978 *West Germany 2–3 Austria*
You can count on good old Berti. Austria hadn't beaten their rivals in 47 years and West Germany fancied their chances of winning and getting to the final. Then keeper Maier drops a cross and Berti deftly manages to back heel it into the net. It was his 96th international but he never played another.

2. Tommy Boyd 1998 *Scotland 1–2 Brazil*
Perhaps he just couldn't stand living in the shadow of the ex-*Magpie* presenter. Maybe the idea of Scotland getting a decent result in a World Cup game was too much to handle. Or just possibly, he was unsettled by the devil stare of Alan Hansen. Whatever, the cack-footed defender hilariously ran a harmless ball into the net and the tartan dream was in tatters again.

3. Pablo Escobar 1994 *Columbia 1–2 USA*
All the talented defender did was turn a cross into his own net – it wasn't as if the rest of the team weren't being played off the park. Ten days later he was shot dead in the Columbian city of Medellin. To think some people thought it was cruel that Phil Neville was made to go and play at Everton.

4. Jimmy Dickinson 1954 *England 4–4 Belgium*
Now, 'Gentleman Jim' had never put a foot wrong before, but boy did he blow it here. Nat Lofthouse's thunderbolt shot off the crossbar in extra-time had finally looked to settle a great yo-yo game. But Jim had to have the last say. Just two minutes later, with no-one around him for miles, he nods in an innocuous free-kick for a Belgian equaliser. Fortunately, we forgive a little better than the Columbians; Jim was given an MBE in 1964.

5. Josef Barmos 1982 *England 2–0 Czechoslovakia*
Paul Mariner's low cross was deflected by the unlucky Czech past his own keeper to secure England's victory. Mariner tried to claim it but everyone knew he could only ever score off his shin or his arse. Better still, the desperate Czech keeper, who had also made a complete balls-up for England's first goal, was called Semen. Feel free to insert your own joke here.

CHAPTER 3
IT'S A FUNNY OLD GAME

55 YEARS OF HURT: PLUCKY SCOTLAND'S ◉◉◉◉◉◉◉ PROUD WORLD CUP RECORD

The wonderful Tartan Army; those canny managers Stein, Ferguson, er… Vogts; ferocious competitors like Mackay and Bremner; footballing genius in Cooke, Baxter, Dalglish – but would you believe Scotland have never got beyond the opening round of the World Cup Finals? Of course, you would. But if you want to revel in some details, read on…

1950 DID NOT QUALIFY
Scotland 0–1 England. The nightmare begins. At Hampden Park 133,000 grown men cry as Roy Bentley puts England into the World Cup in Brazil.

1954 DID NOT QUALIFY
Scotland 2–4 England. Just a few months after England had been taken apart by the Magnificent Magyars, they journeyed north to do the same to the Scots; Tom Finney weaving his magic to deny the auld enemy a trip to Switzerland.

1958 WORLD CUP FINALS – Sweden – Eliminated in Group Stage
Their first World Cup – and Scotland set out their stall. Hopes cruelly raised by a draw with Yugoslavia; goalkeeping mistakes throw away the match against Paraguay and a spineless final game against France finds them on the plane home without a win to their name.

1961 DID NOT QUALIFY
Scotland 2–4 Czechoslovakia. This was surely their moment. A great team – including Paddy Crerand, Dennis Law, John White, Ian St John and Jim Baxter – faced the Czechs in Brussels in a play-off qualifier. Eight minutes to go and Scotland lead 2–1 only to blow it, regal style. Hard luck – the Czechs made it all the way to the final in Chile.

1966 DID NOT QUALIFY
England were really going to get it this time – in their 'aen backyard' as well. After a 1–0 win over Italy at Hampden Park, Scottish supporters already had one piss-stained leg on Wembley Way. See Naples and die they say – and they did, 0–3. Dream over. Still, Italy went on to lose to North Korea – how could Scotland have topped that?

1970 DID NOT QUALIFY

As befitting self-proclaimed World Champions (after they beat England in a friendly in 1967!), Scotland thrashed Cyprus 8–0 and when they were holding the World Cup finalists, West Germany, 2–2 with 10 minutes to go, a trip to Mexico looked on the cards. Oh dear. Another late goal and the dream was stashed away for another four years.

1974 WORLD CUP FINALS – Eliminated in Group Stage

After a comfortable victory over Zaire, a famous draw with competition favourites Brazil and a last–gasp equaliser against Yugoslavia, Scotland were well set for... watching the rest of the tournament at home. The only unbeaten team in the tournament, but hey! Who remembers?

1978 WORLD CUP FINALS – Eliminated in Group Stage

Ally's Army hit South America in style – thrashed by Peru, held by mighty Iran and Willie Johnson was sent home after taking stimulants. But when Archie Gemmill made it 3-1, the small matter of beating the brilliant Holland by three goals suddenly seemed possible. Unfortunately it woke the Dutch up and all that was left were the cries of the Tartan Army's "We wan our monnae back!".

1982 WORLD CUP FINALS – Eliminated in Group Stage

Scotland's greatest World Cup triumph. A shaky 5–2 victory over football giants New Zealand, a late equaliser against Russia and a 1–0 victory over the great Brazil. Well it would have been 1–0 if it had ended after 18 minutes, but as Graeme Souness said, the goal just upset them, and a series of four trademark Brazilian goals destroyed the boys in blue. Scotland came home but, for once, not in disgrace.

1986 WORLD CUP FINALS – Eliminated in Group Stage

Seven shots on target in three matches. Strachan aside, the rest were atrocious, especially Nicol, who missed an open goal against 10-man Uruguay that would have seen them through to the next round. Still, we enjoyed the five minutes in which they led against West Germany.

1990 WORLD CUP FINALS – Eliminated in Group Stage

While England remembers Gazza and co's exploits, Scotland cherish manager Andy Roxborough's "we have nothing to fear from Costa Rica". A hilarious defeat to the Central American no-hopers found Scotland living on hope in the final game against Brazil. For 80 minutes they

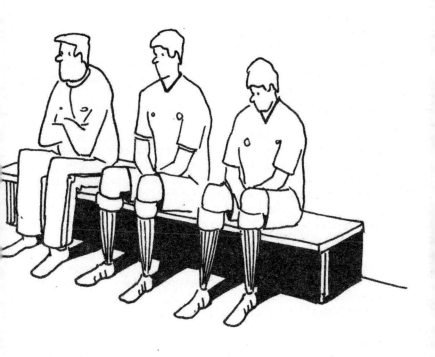

See no victory, feel no victory… a bit like
Scotland in the World Cup Finals.

clung on, only, once again, to have the Xpelair of fate suck away the scent of glory.

1994 DID NOT QUALIFY
Only managing to beat Malta and Estonia (helped by the fact the Estonian team didn't turn up!), Scotland even managed to make Graham Taylor's awful England look good.

1998 WORLD CUP FINALS – Eliminated in Group Stage
Where have we heard this before? After a braveheart defeat to eventual finalists Brazil (beaten by a not-funny-at-all own goal by Tommy Boyd) and a sterling draw with Norway, Scotland had real hopes of qualifying THIS TIME. Cue the whining bagpipes – or was that Alan Hansen in the studio? – as they crumble against the dashing Moroccans.

2002 DID NOT QUALIFY
If you didn't laugh, well, you're probably Scottish, because everyone in England enjoyed the miserablists choking again. This time in Belgium, it was their only defeat of the qualifiers but enough to make the Korea/Japan finals poorer for the absence of Christian Dailly, Billy Dodds and Don Hutchinson... somehow we got by.

2006 DID NOT QUALIFY
It's too delicious. Watching the total incompetency of Berti Vogts' team who struggled to match Moldova was fun; but the revival under Walter Smith followed by the inevitable defeat to Belarus was lick-smackingly delicious.

Never mind, there'll be another chance in four years...

THE WORLD CUP'S LITTLE FRIENDS ⚽⚽⚽⚽⚽⚽⚽⚽⚽⚽⚽⚽⚽

You've probably seen Goleo VI (Go Leo… Gole 06… geddit?) by now. He's the crazy lion-type mascot representing the 2006 tournament. The cheeky lion describes himself as having 'the looks of Lothar Matthaus, the elegance of Diego Maradona and the all-round ability of Oliver Bierhoff!' He never mentions the neck of Peter Crouch, the ugly mug of Oliver Kahn and the irritation factor of Craig Bellamy. And, though no one seems to mention it, he's got no shorts or pants. Exactly what is he saying to our kids? But wait, there's more… He's got a companion, Pille, a talking football with verbal diarrhoea, that presumably Goleo likes to volley right in his tiresome gob.

Let's not forget, the lion is the symbolic animal of ENGLAND (see World Cup Willie below). Isn't there a more suitable animal for the Germans? What about Flyio – the dying fly that wriggles in agony at the slightest touch. Or Wombo, the flying wombat that takes a leap when it nears the penalty area?

Of course Goleo takes his place in a long line of crap mascots…

1966 England: *World Cup Willie*
The original, and best, mascot and the original lion, he was named before Carry-On double entendres so no one tittered. With a Rod Stewart-style mod haircut and an action kicking style, he appeared to be saying "Cool baby!"

1970 Mexico: *Juanito*
No wonder the little lad looked unhappy. His shirt is too small and his large sombrero covers most of his face. He's brought a ball as if it's the only way he's going to get a game. Seems to be saying: "Go easy. I'm from a third world country."

1974 West Germany: *Tip and Tap*
Two rosy-faced boys fresh out of special school have managed to squeeze into the same torn shirt. As they gormlessly wave, you can only imagine they are crying "Come and be my friend… I can tie my own shoelaces and everything."

1978 Argentina: *Gauchito*
Somehow we are supposed to realize that the sweet-faced boy is Argentinian by the fact he has a neckerchief and appears to be carrying

a giant spoon. Thank heavens he has 'Argentina 78' written on his shirt.
Like a ten-year-old Robbie Savage his studs-up challenge does rather
belie his cherubic smile.

1982 Spain: *Naranjito*
A giant orange. Enough said.

1986 Mexico: *Pique*
This is more like it. A chilli pepper with a sombrero and Zapata
moustache – if only they'd completed the stereotype with a bottle of
tequila. Still, he does have the biggest ball of them all.

1990 Italy: *Ciao*
Italy – home of stylish design. So what do we get? Three pipe-cleaners
haphazardly fixed together with a ball for a head. Are these really the
people who brought us Ferrari, Armani, Maldini?

1994 USA: *Striker*
As usual our transatlantic cousins show they just don't understand the
game. A perfect Disney animal with a sensible name. Cowboys, eagles,
buffalo, cheerleaders, stars and stripes... what do they choose? A dog
extra from Huckleberry Hound.

1998 France: *Footix*
Word got about that the French were designing a footballing cock – but
fans were ultimately disappointed with the sub-Asterix chicken in a
jump-suit. No points for 'Frenchness', but he does have the look of
Barthez after one of his balls-ups.

2002 Korea/Japan: *Kaz, Ato & Nik*
From the home of the most imaginative cartoons ever, come three
ugly 'Spheriks' representing energy particles in the atmosphere. Coach
Ato seems to have lost the other nine players of the 'good' Atmo team
which want to bring excitement to the World Cup as opposed to the
Nulmos, who prefer a negative and unpleasant atmosphere... Did anyone
understand what they were on about? Bring back the giant orange.

The Germans rejected Leaping Salmon
Boy as a mascot for the Finals.

♥♥♥ "THERE ARE NO MINNOWS IN WORLD FOOTBALL"

Who is the worst national team in the world? From where we're standing we'd be looking at possibly Liechtenstein (126th), the Faroe Islands (134th) maybe San Marino (157th) – but if Sven and his men (9th) ventured out of Europe, he'd find much bigger banana skins than Northern Ireland (ranked 104th – between Malawi and Cyprus) to slip over.

In fact there are over 200 FIFA affiliated nations in the official rankings, so Scotland (62nd) have someway to fall yet. Chances are it'll take another few managers of the calibre of Berti Vogts to make them the 'Worst Country in the World Cup Final'.

In 2002, on the very same day that Brazil and Germany fought it out in Tokyo, a FIFA sanctioned game between the two lowest rank nations in the world was taking place deep in the Himalayas. Bhutan (202nd) were clear favourites with home advantage, a higher rank than their opponents and even fielding a professional who played in the Indian leagues. Minnows Montserrat, with a population of 5,000 and eight of their players down with altitude sickness and viral infection, were defeated 4–0 and officially received the title of Worst Nation in the World.

Four years later, Montserrat still lurk near the bottom of the table (202nd), while Bhutan (189th) are right up there with giants of the game like Somalia and Macau. Instead, this year could find the mighty Guam (204th) and American Samoa (205th) battling it out. It could be a close one. Neither team have ever beaten FIFA opposition (although American Samoa still bask in their victory over Wallis and Futuna Islands in 1983) and while Guam suffered a 21–0 defeat by North Korea in 2005, American Samoa still haven't got over the 31–0 pasting by Australia in 2001.

REALITY REF ◉◉◉◉◉◉◉◉◉◉◉◉◉◉◉◉◉◉◉◉◉◉◉◉◉◉◉◉◉

England's nemesis, Kim Milton Nielsen – the ref who sent off Beckham in 1998 (for effeminately kicking Simone) and Rooney in 2005 (for sarcastic clapping!) – entered *Vild Med Dans*, Danish television's version of *Strictly Come Dancing* – the show that has d-rated ballroom celebrities dancing in front of z-list judges.

The dandified Dane – hogging the limelight as usual – nonsensically compared dancing to refereeing, saying: "The movement is similar and you have to run a lot." Trying to look cool in his untied bow-tie, he made as much of a pig's ear of his time on the dancefloor as he does on the pitch. Judge Margerthe Laxholm said: "He turned up, there's not much more to say." And the public duly rated his performance as completely incompetent... So there is some connection with his refereeing.

Now we're just waiting to see Graham Poll having rats tuck into his goolies in *I'm a Celebrity* or Urs Meier (who put England out of their Euro 2004 quarter-final) get lumbered with that chav wife from *Wife Swap*.

'THE NEW PELE'

So Brazil's Robinho is the new 'new' Pele? Well, he's Brazilian so that helps, he wears their number 10 shirt and even Pele has called him 'the new me'. But hasn't the 'new Pele' tag been a little overused ever since Edson Arantes do Nascimento got chaired off in his last game for New York Cosmos? Let's see how close the pretenders have come.

ROBINHO
Is the new Pele because: He's great, he's from the same club and he looks a bit like him
Nationality: Brazilian
Nickname: 'New Pele'
Clubs: Santos, Real Madrid
Shirt Number: 10
Attributes: Showboater, goalscorer
Also remembered for: Remains to be seen
Pele Points: 94/100

ADEBELE PELE
Was the new Pele because: He was black, skilful and from a poor background
Nationality: Ghanaian
Nickname: 'African Pele'
Clubs: 1860 München, Marseille
Shirt Number: 10
Attributes: Skilful goalscorer
Also remembered for: Being a FIFA big nob
Pele Points: 87/100

EDUARD STRELTSOV
Was the new Pele because: He was around at the same time and the Soviets wanted one
Nationality: Russian
Nickname: 'Russian Pele'
Clubs: Moscow Torpedo
Shirt Number: 9
Attributes: Abundant talent, his heel pass – still bears his name in Russia
Also remembered for: Being sent to Siberia for refusing to join CSKA or Dinamo Moscow
Pele Points: 85/100

WAYNE ROONEY
Was the new Pele because: Sven told us he was after Euro 2004
Nationality: English
Nickname: 'New Pele'
Clubs: Everton, Manchester United
Shirt Number: 9
Attributes: Great all-round skill, superb goalscorer
Also remembered for: Being king of the chavs
Pele Points: 81/100

PELE

Nationality: Brazilian

Nickname: Pele

Clubs: Santos, New York Cosmos

Shirt Number: 10

Attributes: Incredible skill, team player, goalscorer

Also remembered for: Being a football ambassador and advertising Viagra

Pele Points: 100/100

ZICO

Was the new Pele because: Brazil were desperate for another one

Nationality: Brazilian

Nickname: 'The white Pele'

Clubs: Flamengo, Udinese

Shirt Number: 10

Attributes: Fantastic playmaker when he could be bothered, lousy penalty taker

Also remembered for: Managing Japan in Germany 06

Pele Points: 87/100

JEAN CARLOS CHERA

Is the new Pele because: He's got fantastic skills

Nationality: Brazilian

Nickname: Anderson

Clubs: Parana Sports Athletics Association

Shirt Number: 10

Attributes: Thunderbolt shot, good with both feet, does his homework before tea.

Famous for: Being touted around Europe and he's only nine

Pele Points: 73/100

Honourable mentions to: Neh Lamteh, a Ghanaian player (now untraceable), nicknamed 'the new Pele' after his dazzling performance at the under-17 world championship in Scotland in 1987; Colin Harvey, Everton's 'White Pele', who failed to make England's 1970 World Cup team; Michel Platini, 'the French Pele', good, but nothing like him; Andreas Moller, 'the German Pele' – I suppose they had to have one somewhere; Norwich City and Republic of Ireland's Gary Doherty, 'the ginger Pele' (one fears irony is at play here) and Amarildo, the first 'white Pele', who replaced him in the Brazilian team after Edson had been kicked out of the 1962 World Cup.

◉◉◉◉SCOTLAND – KINGS OF THE WORLD (FOR A MONTH)

Scottish fans are insistent that in defeating World Cup winners England in 1967, they became 'World Champions'. An interesting if ridiculous claim. Indeed, by their own curious logic, Scotland's defeat to the Soviet Union, less than a month later, meant they had one of the shortest reigns ever.

Supposing the 'World Championship' did pass from nation to nation in 'boxing Champion' fashion, The Rec. Sport Soccer Statistics Foundation has charted each holder of the crown. Assuming England as original champions, the title passes around the home nations – even Wales! – until 1939 when England lose it to Yugoslavia. After World War II, the 'championship' is dominated by South American nations before England regain it by beating holders Germany in the World Cup Final in 1966. A whole year passed before the celebrated Scottish triumph.

England would take their rightful place again with two victories over Germany: the Alan Hudson-inspired 2–0 win in 1975 and the 1-0 defeat of the old rivals in Euro 2000 (we passed the crown on to Romania three days later). But despite the roll of honour passing through virtually every football playing country – including Netherlands Antilles (1963), Israel (1994) and Angola (2000) – it never returned to the land of the haggis.

At the end of 2005, the illustrious title belonged to Scotland's fellow World Cup absentees Nigeria after their 5-1 demolition of holders Zimbabwe. Any chance of arranging a friendly, Walter?

For more details, see the RSSSF website at **http://www.rsssf.com**

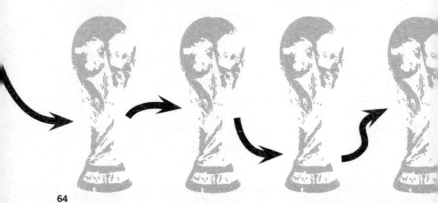

THE GREATEST PLAYERS NEVER TO PLAY AT ⊙⊙⊙⊙⊙⊙⊙⊙ A WORLD CUP

There's going to be some great footballing talent on display in Germany. But for every Phil Neville who goes, there is a Ryan Giggs watching it on TV with his slippers and cocoa. For every Torsten Frings writhing around in mock agony, there is a Nolberto Solano lying on a beach in the Maldives. So who are the greatest never to grace the tournament?

Alfredo Di Stefano – Through injury, FIFA rules or non–qualification, the great striker managed to miss the big one, despite playing for Argentina, Columbia and Spain.

George Best – Bestie had the misfortune to play with a bunch of no-hopers. However, when Northern Ireland qualified in 1982, George claimed Billy Bingham made an 11th-hour plea for him to get fit enough to take part – by that point, however, his sole exercise was getting from the saloon bar to the snug.

Ryan Giggs – The flying winger was unable to inspire his Welsh colleagues to the finals. Perhaps if he'd bothered playing a few more friendlies with them, he might have at least known their names.

Eric Cantona – Insulting the manager, attacking fans, offending the French FA all meant 'King' Eric the Great missed every World Cup. Even as a spectator in 1994 he was in all sorts of trouble. He did, however, coach France to their victorious beach football World Cup in 2005.

David Ginola – November 1993, France vs Bulgaria, injury time. Ginola, in full showman mode, loses possession. Bulgaria break upfield and score. A great France team would miss the finals and the lacquered poodle's international career was finished.

Duncan Edwards – He was a star in England's 1958 Cup qualifying but was killed in the Munich air crash before the finals. Might he have overshadowed Pele and taken England to glory?

George Weah – Great player, might make a good President – but it would have taken a miracle for Liberia to qualify.

CHAPTER 4
HOSTING YOUR OWN WORLD CUP FINALS

HOW MUCH HAS YOUR GIRLFRIEND LEARNED ABOUT THE WORLD CUP?

Try these questions for size on your other half...

1. What made you realize there is a World Cup on?
a) There are fewer people in the shops.
b) My boyfriend is spending more time at home.
c) They've moved Wednesday's *Coronation Street* again.

2. What makes you interested in watching?
a) I fancy Frank Lampard.
b) I fancy the whole Italian team.
c) I got Ecuador in the office sweepstake and want them to win.

3. How long do you think it will go on for?
a) 32 days. The bloody wallchart is up on the bedroom wall.
b) Until England get knocked out – then who cares.
c) Forever – at least it seems like it.

4. Sven-Goran Eriksson is...
a) An overpaid, oversexed Tefal-head.
b) Norwegian Prime Minister.
c) The owner of IKEA.

5. How far can England go in the tournament?
a) They'll be knocked out by a little team like Greenland or Brazil.
b) China.
c) They'll be beaten by Arsenal in the final.

6. What are 4–4–2, 3–5–1 or 4–1–2–2–1?
a) Becks' nanny's phone number.
b) The IQ of each of the players.
c) The length of a football pitch in yards.

7. What is the offside rule?
a) The salt cellar must be nearer the goal than the pepper pot or the vinegar.
b) It's something to do with the boys who get the ball back.
c) Who cares? You patronising sexist pig.

Q 8. That Wayne Rooney just needs a good...
a) ... slap round his bloated fat face.
b) ... seeing-to by an older woman.
c) ... through ball to set him up for his hat-trick.

Q 9. Who would you like to win the World Cup?
a) England. Then can we pack the whole game in?
b) Brazil. Their Samba football is sexy (or so it said in the *TV Times*).
c) Canada. It'd be nice for them – they don't win much.

Q 10. Who is the coach of the German team?
a) Franz Beckhambauer.
b) The one with the smile and the Beetle.
c) Arsenal Wenger.

Q 11. Totti and Toni are...
a) Hairdressers on the high street.
b) The new cartoon on *CBeebies*.
c) Ineffectual Italian strikers who are let down by the lack of opportunities created by an ultra-defensive midfield system.

What the answers say about your girlfriend.

Whether she got them right or wrong, she's not interested, right? She might be being nice to you, feeling sorry for you, fancy you or be hoping you buy her a new pair of shoes, but she really couldn't care less whether England march on to the final, much less whether Saudi Arabia beat the Czech Republic. And, if by some remote chance, she does get interested, it's even worse, as she'll...

- Invite her friends round to watch it and witter on through the whole game.
- Turn the whole thing into a dinner party with food themed around whoever England are playing.
- Annoy you by asking obvious questions such as "Which club does Wayne Rooney play for?"
- Make you look stupid by asking 'difficult' questions such as "Which club does Luke Young play for?"
- Get bored and ask if she could flick over to see *Big Brother* at half-time.
- Get bored and ring her mum during the penalty shoot-out.

The Mexican wave – symbolic of
celebration in crap sports – finally
made its way to football.

))◉◉◉IT ISN'T THAT GOOD

Five reasons why, after the initial euphoria has worn off, you might find yourself channel-hopping, reading a good book, even wallpapering the spare room – just to escape the tournament.

You only get one decent match in ten in the group stage.

Oh great, it's Ecuador against Switzerland tonight – a set of players you've never heard of and a standard that looks a bit like the Conference. Come to think of it, doesn't the Ecuadorian winger play for Stevenage Borough?

The supposed sell-out matches turn out to be empty stadiums.

Rows and rows of empty seats, a group of schoolboys in the corner chanting in irritating high-pitched voices and an atmosphere that makes Highbury look like the Maracana.

Boring game, boring extra time, boring penalties.

Some matches are incapable of raising a heartbeat no matter what happens: the midfield stalemate, the incapable strikers, the endless stoppages for broken fingernails – by extra time you've lost the will to live.

Slow, slow, slow-slow-slow.

The continental sides may be full of marvellously technical players, but couldn't they hurry it up a little. "Just look at the skill with which he passes the ball along the back line – for the umpteenth time." What you'd give for a good old hoof up t' field.

After England, everything is an anti-climax.

You know the scene. England have just won on penalties, you're on a massive high and eagerly await the next match: Croatia vs Sweden. As much as you try it's just not got that fizz. You give it 20 minutes. Nothing happens. You go down the pub.

It was an important goal but, as celebrations went, recreating the death scene from *Richard III* seemed a little over the top.

BUT... Don't give up. Here's what you're missing on the other channels:

Big Brother 48

It's down to a transvestite, a yapping bloke who, if he was a dog, would be put down, a screaming queen and an Alzheimer's sufferer who wandered in by accident.

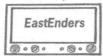

EastEnders

Pauline's got enough on her plate, the chav family are nicking stuff, someone's lost a baby and Dot's going on about God again. Warms the cockles don't it? No.

You Are What You Vomit

Fat people are made to swim through sick until they agree to live on carrots and cabbage and cut down on the cigs.

Don't Go Out Dressed Like That

Menopausal women with severe depression are shown that all you need to do to cheer yourself up is put on a dress with a plunging neckline and throw out those dowdy cardigans.

Moving Back In

Two poncey estate agents help people buy back the houses that two years ago they sold to go and start a new life in the Dordogne.

CableVision Blockbuster Film

They really think they are going to tempt you away with some film you can get on DVD for 99p down the market.

When defending a free kick, players
hold on to what's most dear to them...

WALLCHART ALERT!

So, wallcharts, who needs them? You do, you've had one since you were ten and have no intention of stopping now. You know you'll be out there buying one in plenty of time for the opening match to be ceremonially filled in. So it's time to establish some ground rules.

1. It's fine to leave the chart unfilled. But once you start, you have to finish. No-one will be impressed with a chart where you've bothered with the first two games and then left the rest blank.

2. Decide in advance how much information you are going to include: scores are essential and scorers a useful addition; half-time scores are a mite pretentious and attendances, referees, bookings and sendings-off are just asking a little too much.

3. Consider the texture. Are you happy with a pullout from a newspaper? The biro can tear the paper, a felt-tip will blot and it will go yellow by the final. Then again, a glossy finish looks great when you find it in the attic ten years later, but try filling in the scores with a biro when it's up on the wall. It's a personal thing.

4. Where will you put it? By the TV is ideal for reference during games, but the kids can write on it and the wife is able to arrange for her parents to come for lunch during the England vs Italy match. If you put it in the bathroom, just put it far out of the range of those taking a quick pee during an injury break.

5. Avoid the workplace wallchart. They are unreliable, as some Scotsman will make England's opponents have a rugby score or some wag will manipulate it to make Togo appear in the final.

The opposition were forced to come up
with innovative ways of dealing with
Peter 'The Grinch' Crouch.

⊃◕◕◕CALL YOURSELF AN EXPERT?

They'll be like unpaying guests in your house for three weeks so you better get used to them. Ever since Mexico '70, when the nation hung on every Brian Clough word of wisdom and desperately tried to make out what Mick Channon was going on about, the TV stations have decided what we need are three old pros – now 'pundits' – on a couch, wittering on about offside decisions. The lucky 'expert' will get to sit in the gantry next to Motty, Pearcey or Tylery and say "Yes, you're right there" over and over again. In the case of Graeme Le Saux or Trevor Brooking this extends to explaining what is happening while we watch the slow motion replay. "He's gone past his man there, got a good cross..." I know. I'm watching it for Christ's sake!

The exposure of the World Cup, of course, gives your pundit a chance to become a household name and completely mispronounce everyone elses. It is difficult to get your tongue round some of the more obscure nations' players but you feel Jack Charlton might even struggle with 'Joe Cole'.

For the TV channels, picking the team is as difficult a job as Sven's, but get the formation right – fill your time with ad breaks or goal of tournament competitions – and before you know it it's back to Dortmund for a, hopefully, more exciting second half.

The Presenter
"...back to the studio". It's vital for our host to strike the right tone: sombre, with a glimmer of hope if England have just let in a goal; optimistic but not cocky if they are leading. Lynam was the master, Lineker looks like he's been worn out pretending to laugh at Rory McGrath's jokes, while Logan has a lot to learn. May be required to separate aggressive pundits, come up with god-awful puns or wake Peter Reid.

The Heavyweight Pundit
We're looking for tactical guidance, a hint to the subtle rhythm changes of the game – a bit more than "I like the look of that big fellow at the back". It helps if you have a handy catchphrase like Alan Hansen's 'shocking defence' or easy access to a table of formations like Terry Venables. ("That's a 4–3–3 mutating into a 4–2–1–2".) If you run out of things to say, pick a fight with one of the other guests. Hansen usually

takes them to task over the role of the holding player but their choice of tie or "looking at me in a funny way" can also lead to friction.

The Steady Pro
They've been there, done it… been dropped… tried management… been sacked. Their job is to provide, with as dull a drone as possible, a pro's eye view. It might seem coincidental but Townsend, Reid, Dixon etc have been trained to speak for exactly the time it takes to get a beer from the fridge and pour it without getting too much of a head.

The Light Touch
While Peter Schmeichel's comic nose, Gordon Strachan's incoherent rants or Gazza's disintegrating grip on the English language might make it worth sitting through 45 minutes of Saudi Arabia vs Serbia and Montenegro, true comic genius is provided by the likes of Ian Wright and Ally McCoist – if you're eight years old.

The Pitch-Side Reporter
Short of cleaning the bog after Ron Atkinson has been in, it's about the worst job on the team. Involves analysing substitutes' buttock shifting to see who's coming on next, or – and Gabriel Clarke is an expert here – peering over the physio's shoulder to proclaim: "There's a lot of blood." Finally, who can forget Garth Crooks 'informing' a bemused Sven that England were through, after the group stages of the 2002 finals?

The Foreigner
Just as the continental touch has enlivened the domestic game, so has the introduction of Gullit, Vialli, Cudicini and others changed the whole panel game. Technically more adept and tactically aware, they pass their thoughts accurately and economically – though many viewers miss the raw excitement of British pundits such as Sam Allardyce who'd toss wild comments into the area willy-nilly.

The Former England Manager
In the good old days discredited England managers were chained in Leicester Square for people to throw old fruit at them. Now they appear on TV to spout rubbish at us. Like Bobby 'I discovered Ronaldo, you know' Robson (of course you did, Bobby, now drink up your hot milk). And when will someone shut Graham Taylor up with the words: "Carlton. Palmer. 18. Caps!"

WHERE TO WATCH THAT ENGLAND MATCH

1. The Pub

Advantages: A good atmosphere, accessible alcohol, hordes of like-minded souls willing the team on. None of the distractions of home.

Disadvantages: You can't get a good view of the screen, you've drunk too much so you're seeing double, you've got some Scotsman bitterly supporting some country he's never heard of just because they are playing England and in the ten minutes it's taken you to go to the loo you've missed two goals, a sending off and the shot of Mick Jagger singing the national anthem.

2. The Living Room

Advantages: You've got your own beer in the fridge, your carefully-selected mates, a kitchen full of snacks and a loo where you can leave the door open and still hear what's going on.

Disadvantages: You run out of beer. The child you've dreamed of watching the game with gets bored after 20 minutes and starts screaming for his Harry Potter DVD. Your wife's mother rings during the penalty shoot-out and none of the family are talking to you because you kicked the cat.

3. At Work

Advantages: They've put on free beer and hired a massive screen. The girl you fancy is impressed by your knowledge of Owen Hargreaves and your boss is listening in admiration of your tactical understanding.

Disadvantages: They've only bought supermarket lager; the managers are in their swivel chairs while everyone else has to perch on the desks; the girl you fancy thinks you're a bore going on about Owen Hargreaves and your boss isn't impressed by the way you belched the national anthem.

4. In a Hotel Room

Advantages: It's just you. The phone's off the hook, the mini-bar is full and you can lie on your bed, have a bath or pace around the room and still see the screen.

Disadvantages: You miss half the match because you can't work out which channel they've put BBC1 on. You have an immediate need to discuss the game and spend a fortune ringing your mates in the pub on exorbitant hotel rates. You've emptied the mini-bar – even the miniature Baileys – and it's not even half-time.

CHAPTER 5
GERMANY!

THE ROCKY ROAD TO GERMANY ⊙⊙⊙⊙⊙⊙⊙⊙⊙⊙⊙⊙⊙

The great thing about the qualifiers are the nuisance teams, those nations who haven't got a hope of qualifying – like Scotland – but still put a spanner in the works of teams with loftier ambitions. This series of games has thrown up the usual selection of humorous results – and, of course, an England embarrassment.

Northern Ireland 1–0 England
While the multi-millionaires jogged around Windsor Park like they didn't want to get their over-sponsored boots dirty, a selection of ginger-haired, potato-faced or pot-bellied workhorses kicked them up the arse and where it hurt most.

Mauritania 2–1 Zimbabwe
FIFA believed Mauritania was a country invented by *Dynasty* writers in the 80s and only put them in the draw for a laugh. Imagine Robert Mugabe's surprise when Zimbabwe (ranked 49th by FIFA) got beat by Joan Collins, Linda Evans and the rest.

New Zealand 2–4 Vanuatu
The Kiwis, World Cup qualifiers in 1982, had struggled to beat the Solomon Islands, but at least they'd heard of them. Vanuatu (named after a *Star Trek* planet), had failed to score in their games against Fiji and the Solomans and faced five matches in nine days – with only one pair of boots each.

The Maldives 0–0 South Korea
Citing the old 'no minnows in world football' line, the 2002 World Cup semi-finalists took a strong squad – including four European-based players – to play a team who had never really recovered from a 17-goal defeat by Iran in the 1998 World Cup qualifiers. They returned to a barrage of 'overpaid', 'arrogant', 'benders in night clubs' headlines all too familiar to the 'four European-based players'.

Liberia 1–0 Mali
Did the Liberians taunt the Malian supporters with their favourite "Schush!" chant? Whatever. The African nations semi-finalists – Kanoute, Sissoko, Djimi Traore, er.. that's all I've heard of – fell to the country ranked 134th in the world. In Africa, that was a big deal – honest.

Scotland 1–1 Italy
They may be a once great footballing nation now forever destined to scrape results with plucky performances, but Italy really shouldn't be throwing easy points like this away. Italy coach Marcello Lippi said: "We were very surprised by Kenny Miller who played very well." Anyone who has watched the lumbering Wolves forward would surely sympathise.

⦿⦿⦿⦿COMMENTATOR CLICHÉ B I N G O

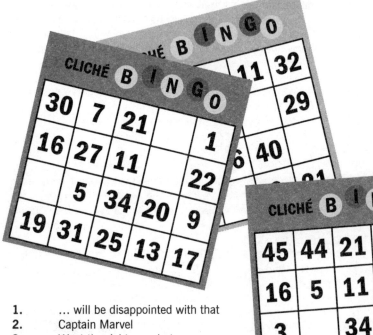

1. … will be disappointed with that
2. Captain Marvel
3. Went the right way, but
4. Group of death
5. Samba soccer
6. A little naive
7. It's a lottery
8. Single moment of magic
9. German efficiency
10. He's walking rather gingerly
11. Just a spot of handbags
12. It's game on now
13. If there's one guy you want
14. Early doors
15. All credit to…
16. Setting their stall out
17. Asking questions of the … defence

18. You'd put your mortgage on him scoring
19. Great touch for a big man
20. Something to tell their grandchildren about
21. ...feel that it's just a matter of time before
22. The best possible start
23. It beyond ...'s reach
24. Take it one game at a time
25. Into row Z
26. Pulling the strings
27. Cultured left foot
28. He always gives 110 per cent
29. He's got a great engine
30. Playing in the hole
31. No such thing as minnows
32. Didn't look like there was much contact though
33. Ouch, that's gotta hurt
34. Looked worse than it was

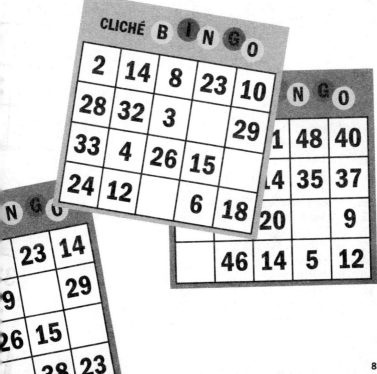

◗◉◉◉HALF-TIME CHUCKLE

When the Angolan team met up for their pre-tournament training camp there was much to talk about. Players had travelled from teams spread across the world and were eager to catch up on each other's progress. The talented midfielder who had gone to play in England, however, seemed particularly down.

"What's the matter?" asked a teammate. "You had the best move... a great club, superb manager, a team full of internationals."

"I know" said his friend. "It was going well. I'd scored on my debut and was just doing my man-of-the match interview when I got a phone call. It turned out that my wife had been mugged, my car set on fire and my son attacked with a machete."

"That's terrible" agreed his mate.
"It's awful. They'd only been in Manchester for a week."

Phillip was prepared to go to any length
to get back in the England team.

●●●●ARE YOU A ROONEY OR AN OWEN?

Q 1. When watching England at home where do you like to sit?
a) Bolt upright in 'Daddy's Armchair'.
b) I can't sit, just pace about nervously.
c) In my favourite designer lazyboy chair.
d) Lying on the sofa within reach of cigarettes and crisps.

Q 2. England are coasting 3–0 up against Ecuador. Your girlfriend wants to watch *Big Brother*. Do you…
a) Let her switch over, the game is effectively over and you only want to keep her happy?
b) Leg it down the pub to catch the final ten minutes?
c) Tell her to get a life or she'll be up for eviction?
d) Throw your dinner at the dog and pack your bags?

Q 3. Slovakia vs Paraguay is on TV. Do you…
a) Settle down to watch it in its entirety?
b) See how it goes before knocking a quick one off?
c) Turn over to see if anyone's getting undressed on *Hollyoaks*?
d) Go down the pub?

Q 4. You are in the pub watching England's quarter-final penalty shoot-out against Germany. Your mobile shows the doctor attending your sick mother is calling. Do you…
a) Leave the pub and take the call?
b) Take the call, stare at the screen and ignore the conversation?
c) Divert the call to voicemail and forget to check the message until the morning?
d) Take the call and give him a running commentary on the game?

Q 5. Your parents have invited their German friends to watch the England vs Germany game. Can you…
a) Sit through the game, politely congratulating them on their team's fine passing moves?
b) Not resist writhing around in agony when they affectionately ruffle your hair?
c) Avoid performing an 'in their face' celebration à la John Cleese, when England score?
d) Manage one minute without hurling abuse at the team, the nation, their history and national dress?

6. What do you like to drink during a tense World Cup match?
a) Nothing. You're constantly dying for the loo as it is.
b) A small glass of Chablis.
c) A mug of tea and a packet of biscuits for each half.
d) Down four pints in the first half hour then spend the rest of the match trying to see just one of everyone.

7. You are watching Scotland play a pre-World Cup friendly against a team who did manage to qualify. Do you...
a) Offer sympathy for their bad luck in not reaching the Finals?
b) Yearn for the days of Bremner, Dalglish, and even Hendry?
c) Admire their plucky spirit and promising mediocre young players as you scratch your genitals?
d) Laugh at the very idea of Fletcher and Dickov playing international football?

8. After their third lily-livered performance England are eliminated from the finals at the group stage. Do you...
a) Accept the inevitable, consider what lessons may be learned and look forward to Euro 2008?
b) Write a letter to the *Daily Telegraph* about overpaid, pampered players?
c) Get drunk and rail at FIFA; referees; weather conditions; Posh Spice and, before climbing into bed in tears, yourself, for not wearing those lucky underpants again?
d) Blame Sven and start an internet petition to invade Sweden?

9. A welcome, if unexpected, sexual opportunity means you are going to miss the start of the England game. Do you...
a) Carry on regardless, thinking you may not get another chance for months and nothing ever happens in the first half-hour (of the football)?
b) Run off, secretly put the video on, but come back to the bedroom with the chocolate spread?
c) Finish off quickly, excusing yourself with a "sorry, that's never happened before"?
d) Put the telly on. The World Cup's only every four years and at least you get sex on your birthday?

10. England are 1–0 down to Argentina in the Second Round. Sven gets Peter Crouch to warm up. Are you...

a) Pleased because he is an honest player with a good touch for a tall man?

b) Forced to admit that, despite his limitations, he provides Sven with a 'Plan B'?

c) Crying out in utter desperation for Jermain Defoe?

d) Throwing cans at the telly, shouting "If I wanted to see a f**ing freak show, I'd go to the circus"?

Mostly As – You are a Michael Owen

You are a responsible, well-grounded member of society – if a little boring. For you a visit to the pole-dancing is down to the village green to see your daughter as this year's May Queen. So humble in victory, so generous in defeat – it's sometimes difficult to know whose side you are on. Would it really do any harm, though, to have a few lagers and tell Raul what you truthfully think of him?

Mostly Bs – You are a Rio Ferdinand

Basically, you're a sound guy but you like to let your hair down a bit. A smart guy who might forget the odd drugs test – that's not a crime is it? Well, in the eyes of the FA maybe. People might call you 'thickie', but who do they come running to when they need a reliable centre half – apart from John Terry? And Sol? And Ledley, and Jonathan and Jamie...

Mostly Cs – You are a David Beckham

You're oh-so-nearly the modern man! Manicured nails, tattoos of your children's names in Chinese, asymmetrical haircuts, an interest in Baudelaire and French 19th Century poetry... but still, it doesn't quite win everyone over. See, we know about the text sex, the awful voice (don't complain, you married it), the tasteless mansion, the white boots...

Mostly Ds – You are a Wayne Rooney

Oh to be so young, tempestuous, bold and utterly charmless. There was a time when you had 'Chav' written on your forehead, but now you've nearly learned to spell it yourself. To you football is just a child's playground – a stunning goal at break-time, a bit of a scrap at lunchtime and a quick one with a granny after school (OK – the last one is stretching the illusion a little). You've got everything to look forward to, but somehow we know you'll find a way to magnificently cock it up.

Awaiting the Magic Sponge
(see Glossary, page 126).

◉◉◉◉UZBEKISTAN PAY THE PENALTY

For Uzbekistan and Bahrain, it was the match of their lives, a two-legged play-off to earn the right to fight over a World Cup place in Germany with Trinidad and Tobago. At 1–0 up in their home leg, all was looking good for the Uzbekis, especially when, after 39 minutes, they converted a penalty that doubled their lead. Or did it?

Japanese referee, Toshimitsu Yoshida, had spotted an Uzbekistan player entering the penalty area before the kick was taken. As every schoolboy knows, the kick should have been re-taken, but this king clot ref gave Bahrain a free-kick. The match finished 1–0.

FIFA, of course, would make sure justice was done – wouldn't it? No. It suspended the referee and ordered the game to be replayed. "The referee stole our second goal and now FIFA is stealing our first goal," said Alisher Nikimbaev, the UFF's head of international relations to no avail. This time Bahrain took the lead and although Uzbekistan, coached by Englishman Bobby Houghton, equalised, the damage had been done.

A 0–0 draw in Bahrain saw the Uzbekis go out on away goals – the most unfairly treated nation ever?

THREE INCHES TO GERMANY ⚽⚽⚽⚽

Despite a few hiccups, Cameroon, Africa's most successful World Cup nation, seemed destined for the 2006 finals. An impressive 3–2 victory in the Ivory Coast had left them only needing to beat Egypt to qualify. Cameroon President Paul Biya had promised generous bonuses for the players if they won. All 40,000 tickets were sold, and each came with a special T-shirt to transform Ahmadou Ahidjo Stadium into a mass of green.

When Rudolf Douala put them ahead in the 20th minute, the match seemed to be going to plan, but Cameroon failed to capitalize and, with just over 10 minutes remaining, the Pharaohs equalised through Mohamed Sawky.

As Ivory Coast were exacting a 3–1 victory in Sudan, the situation was becoming desperate. Cameroon went all-out for a winner, forcing amazing saves and last-ditch blocks from the Egyptians and missing an open goal. Then, with just 30 seconds of the allotted five minutes left, Amr Zaki took a wild swing in the box and Salomon Olembe tumbled theatrically to the ground. Penalty.

There are two versions of what happened next. Eto'o, the African Footballer of the Year, who plays his club soccer for Barcelona, says he was prepared to take the kick but Pierre Wome – whose penalty had won Cameroon's only ever gold medal in the 2000 Olympics – begged to take it. "I went to take it but Wome came up to me and said he was really confident of scoring."

Wome, who plays for Inter Milan, has a slightly different memory of events. "No-one wanted to take that penalty. No-one. Neither Eto'o nor our captain [Rigobert Song], because they knew what could have happened if they missed. I have always had the courage and I went to the spot."

Whatever. Up stepped Wome to rattle his shot low and hard – only to see it come back from the right-hand upright. Cameroon would not qualify. The green-clad fans were devastated: "They wanted to and could have killed me," said the despairing Wome.

⚽⚽⚽⚽ WORLD ASSOCIATION FOOTBALL

Here's what everyone really thinks of everyone else!

Angola – Angry
Argentina – Bitter
Australia – Unsuitable
Bahrain – Bandy
Brazil – Show-offs
Cote d'Ivoire – Naive
Costa Rica – Crazy
Croatia – Fractious
Czech Republic – Alice bandy
Ecuador – Grateful
France – Mealy-mouthed
Germany – Diving
Ghana – Over-physical
Iran – Defensive
Italy – Whinging
Japan – Jammy
Korea Republic – Too clever

Mexico – Lily-livered
Netherlands – Cliquey
Poland – Limited
Portugal – Over-emotional
Paraguay – Do you mean **Uruguay**?
Togo – Endearing
Tunisia – Stilted
Saudi Arabia – Dogged
Serbia and Montenegro – Schizophrenic
Spain – Disappointing
Sweden – Blond
Switzerland – Unemotional
Trinidad and Tobago – Ineffectual
Ukraine – Pasty-faced
USA – Upstarts

⚽⚽⚽⚽ GO TEAM USA!

FIFA ranks the USA as one of the six best teams in the world. Better than Sweden, Spain and, as they might say, Goddammed England. So who have they got better than Rio, Becks and the Roonster? Heck! Who have they got any better than freakin' Phil Neville? We went to ask an American football expert… Unfortunately there aren't any. So instead, American Football commentator (or 'sportscaster') Stud Walzheimer gave us his lowdown on Team USA.

> After striking out at the eight-team play-out stage in the 2002 World Series, Team USA were aiming high for the 2006 Soccerball finals in Germany, Europe. The regional class-qualification selection drew up something like Bermuda Triangle, St Cougar Islands, Texas and Mexico. Dang! It was going to be a tough hog-shoot to emerge head of those standings.
>
> The details of qualification were baffling – but a two-play aggregation against the Rio Grande Chilli-eaters was the highlight of the series. Man, why those Mexicans hate us beats me – most of them live here anyway!
>
> United States hasn't been bested by Mexico since 1999 and hasn't yielded any field-strikes in that span either, but gameday at Columbus Crew found Team USA in stand-down position in the ratings – Mexico with an on-the-road close out of 5–1–1 looking good-to-go. The Coyotes might have had the game iced at intermission, but goal-tender Keller performed big when Mexico's offensive hitman Morales looked sure-fire to convert during first-period additional clockage.
>
> Deep into the third quarter, USA won a violation shot deep in the endzone and Eddie Lewis's looper met the head of defensive blocker Onyewu. Re-entering play off the pole it fell to the unguarded Ralston for a decisive net-shot. Minutes later, from a special endplay, Skip Reyna fed loose man Beasley for a thunderous goal-strike. Two-zip. Despite Frankie Hejduk narrowly avoiding field-eviction and Keller performing a diving hand-save, USA rode safe through to closure.

Pick of the Roster

Kasey Keller

Net Guard KC blanked five straight opponents in qualifying with a shutout streak of 507 minutes.

Landon Donovan

Europe-drafted goal-bagger whose speed-play spells danger anywhere in the endzone.

Eddie Johnson

A huge breakout season for the rookie strikeman with a 4–5 strike rate in the Youth World Cup.

Oguchi Onyewu

At two-ten pounds, 'Gooch' shores up backfield with awesome power and intelligent gameplay.

DaMarcus Beasley

First hitting the roster in 2000, the Fort Wayne playcaller dominates left sideline play.

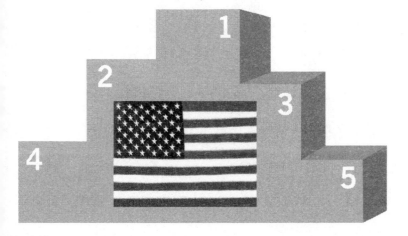

◐◐◐◐GOLDENBOOTS

They'll all be there come June – Ronaldo, Zidane, Owen, even a couple of Championship players – poncing around in their white, red, suede-shade, bronze boots. England's World Cup winning hero Alan Ball is to blame. As if having ginger hair and a squeaky whining voice wasn't enough he was the first to deviate from the standard boot with white monstrosities. Of course, NOW he admits "they were crap, like cardboard, so I got the young apprentices to paint my Adidas boots white. It was great till one day it rained and the black came through."

Nowadays, of course, everyone – even Robbie Savage – is wearing white, so your classier player is looking elsewhere. Enter the David Beckham Limited Edition Predator Pulse, a limited edition of 723 (Becks' England and Real Madrid numbers), at a price of 723 euros (about £500). Each pair comes in a wooden box inspired by an Asian shrine and is accompanied by quotes from Confucius. The silver and red boots, with feng shui symbols sewn into them, are promoted as Beckham's 'yin and yang boots'. Yin and Yang is Japanese for 'b******s'.

Then there's Ronaldinho. The Brazilian with more money than dentistry has had a special pair of boots made for him, including eight ounces of 24-carat gold. They also have a letter R, the number 10 and five gold stars to signify the five World Cups won by Brazil.

ST CRUYFF'S SCHOOL TRIP TO GERMANY 2006 ⊙⊙⊙⊙⊙

HEADMASTER'S LETTER

Dear Parent,

Congratulations. Your boy has been picked to represent the school at the World Cup tournament in Germany. Please make sure they are at the airport in plenty of time for the flight. (Mrs Bergkamp, please put Dennis on the coach at least a week earlier.) In view of previous disappointments, please make sure they understand the following rules:

- Only school uniform to be worn. Please keep the orange to a minimum – last time we lost both Koeman brothers to the Hari Krishnas.
- Players without dreadlocks will find extensions available at the school shop.
- Would Mrs Davids please make sure Edgar leaves his joke shop glasses at home. They weren't funny the first time.
- Please tell your boy not to tease Robben. He has just reached puberty earlier. He is not going bald.
- Games master Mr van Basten's decision is final. Van Nistelrooy and Mackaay will have to accept there is only one number 9 shirt.
- Contrary to the lavatory grafitti, Japp Stam is not 43. This was a cruel rumour put around by former school caretaker Mr Ferguson.
- Boys claiming 4-4-2 is a natural Dutch formation will be sent home.
- We will try to discourage homesickness. Long faces will not be acceptable – except in the case of van Nistelrooy.
- We are not at home to Mr Ego. Boys prone to sulking – I'm looking at you Seedorf – will be locked in their room.
- We are ambassadors for our country. Boys caught smoking normal cigarettes will be made to roll their own.
- Please remember the Germans are our hosts – don't laugh when they go out in the first round.
- Mr van Basten has had confrontations with many parents over his choice of playing style. If you are unhappy with any aspects of the team, please remember your boy could be playing for Belgium.

I wish the boys every success and, hopefully, if we manage a week without in-fighting, tantrums or Robben taking his ball home, we won't come home early again.

Yours,

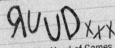

Ruud Gullitt, Head of Games

97

⚽⚽⚽⚽DIVING'S COMING HOME

At last the best actors, divers and cheats in the world are returning to the nation that perfected it. The Germans remain the only country to have won the tournament on a dive – Klinsmann's superb treble twist and ankle clinging performance securing the winning penalty in 1990 – and they are the only country to have their own word for the black art, *Schwalbe*. But has the whole journey into deceit gone too far?

The Actors Association has complained about the use of 'play-acting' on demarcation grounds, suggesting footballers stick to football and let actors get on with their jobs. A spokesperson claimed his profession was already aghast at the quality of some of the players attending this year's finals. Among those criticised were:

Czech midfielder Pavel Nedved

❝ He goes down far too quickly – there's no feeling, no primeval cry from the depths of his soul. Reminiscent of a young Rodney Bewes. ❞

Italian striker Francesco Totti

❝ The school of overblown facial expressions, pleas for his mama and hands clasped in prayer is really so 1970s Fellini. ❞

Dutch Forward Ruud van Nistelrooy

❝ Where is the passion? Where is the truth? Has he spent four years at Drama School pretending to be a tree? No. And my does it show, sweetie. ❞

He did, however, have some complimentary words for France's Robert Pires. "His performance around the edge of the penalty area was totally believable; his marvellous stumble and fall was perfectly complimented by a puppy-eyed innocent appeal and finished off with angry finger-wagging. It was as if Rudi Voller and Marlon Brando had a love child."

In return, 'retaliatory' action has already broken out among the acting profession. At the Olivier Theatre, the Tuesday performance of Tom Stoppard's *Bumpf* saw Martin Jarvis volley home a Frances de la Tour cross just before the interval and at the Criterion, the RSC's *Macbeth* included a new character called Keane who, early doors, cruelly scythed down Banquo with a two-footed tackle.

Meanwhile, reports that Ashley Cole was cut to the quick by *Guardian* Theatre Critic Michael Bilgington's review of his mock-elbow-in-the-face display at the Nou Camp are unconfirmed. Cole was rumoured to have reacted to the charge of his portrayal being 'faux and verging on the pretentious' by spending literally minutes with Richard Briers at the Old Vic.

The Italians weren't taking any
chances with bad refereeing decisions
this time.

⚽⚽⚽⚽THAT'S THE TICKET

A man takes his seat at the World Cup Final. He looks to his left and notices that there is a spare seat in between himself and the next guy.

"Who would ever miss the World Cup Final?" asks the man.

"That was my wife's seat. We have been to the last five World Cup Finals together, but sadly she passed away," explains the guy.

"That's terrible, but couldn't you get another member of the family, friend or someone else to come with you?" asks the man.

"No... They are all at the funeral!"

WHO'S THE B*****D IN THE YELLOW?

At the time of writing, the referee panel for the 2006 World Cup has not been finalised. FIFA aims to both select the best available officials, and in a spirit of inclusion, invite referees from less renowned footballing nations. This guarantees the global audience a superb opportunity to view the arrogant, the prima donnas, the incompetent and the bizarre. The following list is just a guess at who might be officiating.

Scotland: A no-nonsense, prim Presbyterian fond of handing out bookings for shirts not being tucked in and 'looking at me in a funny way'.

Venezuelan: Though only 4 ft 11 ins, he makes his authority known through flamboyant gestures and barking at players in a language they don't understand.

Qatar: Looks the part – smart uniform, handsome moustache, shiny whistle – so why don't any of the players take a blind bit of notice of him?

Luxembourg: Coiffeured hair, manicured hands, orange sun tan, he looks fantastic and doesn't he know it. Even if you don't notice him immediately, he makes sure you will when he gives Ronaldo, Rooney, Ballack etc, a good ten-minute telling off.

Spanish: FIFA's finest. He's done the lot; Champions League finals, Euro finals, meaningless World Club Championships. The players know him, even women sports reporters on Channel Five have heard of him. Players claim he responds to dissent by asking how much *they* got for their last footwear ad.

Italian: Looks very ordinary but exudes extraordinary authority. Having never booked anyone, he is said to have mob contacts with a reputation for breaking metatarsals.

Austria: He has a self-respect problem that he believes can only be solved by flashing a card every three minutes, full-body searches for substitutes' jewellery, and an insistence on free-kicks being taken from within two inches of the infringement.

England: Part-time referee, full time public school Latin teacher and a sadist from birth, he sees the players as naughty schoolboys. Loves lecturing with a wagging finger and condescending smiles. Once gave Rooney lines for expectorating and tried to cane Ashley Cole.

Banangula: An official translation of the rules hasn't yet reached this Pacific island. That hasn't stopped their official from taking part and introducing his own new raft of rules banning heading and encouraging two-footed challenges. He does, however, seem to have a better understanding of the offside law than Graham Poll.

Australia: 'Laissez faire' is the kindest description of his refereeing style. Never known to award a free-kick, he constantly shouts "Get up, it's a man's game, Blue". The players call him Brett and he addresses them as "Cocksucker…"

Bulgaria: There's always one with an eye for the controversial decision. Unexplainable disallowed goals, bizarre penalty decisions, sendings-off that are retracted by FIFA before he's left the pitch and a plethora of fail throws… Far East betting syndicates have begun running spreads on his calls.

✪✪✪✪STADIUM MAYHEM

Germany claims to have built the finest stadiums in World Cup history, but how do they stand in the architectural league? Leading architect Pascal Burritzer* casts an expert eye over some of the specially designed grounds hosting the World Cup games.

Berlin: *Olympiastadion*
An incandescent Prince Charles described it as a 'monstrosity of immense proportions'. Fortunately, he had mistakenly been given a picture of Sepp Blatter. A beautiful construction of metal, glass and polyurethane.

Dortmund: *Westfalenstadion*
Miraculously transformed from an abattoir, this magnificent structure will seat over 80,000 people. Unfortunately, local planning regulations will ensure it returns to its previous function shortly before the stadium hosts the quarter-final.

Frankfurt: *Waldstadion*
The smallest of all the stadiums has had the most corporate support. Of the 40,000 seats, 25,000 are in executive boxes, 12,000 are in the Michelin-starred restaurant and more than 2,000 are reserved for large furry company mascots.

Gelsenkirchen: *Veltins-Arena*
The famous stadium of FC Schalke 04 was built more than 100 years ago. Every proud triumph and heart-rending disappointment seeped into its very foundations, every shout of the crowd was said to echo forever around its magnificent stands. In 2004 they knocked it down and put up this sterile concrete structure.

Hamburg: *AOL Arena*
Here they are boasting the ultimate 'customer' comfort. 'Customers' will be able to order meals, drinks and action replays from an armrest touch-pad. The controversial 'ejector seat' button that evicts the irritating git sitting next to you has, however, been removed on safety grounds.

Hannover: *AWD-Arena*

Cycle parks, organic grass and seats made from recycled plastic make this the most eco-friendly stadium ever constructed. Coaches and those on the subs benches will be required to cycle at a constant 20 rpm to maintain the floodlighting.

Kaiserslautern: *Fritz-Walter-Stadion*

Designed by post-modernist architect Dale Winton, the stadium combines neo-classical columns, art deco paving and Bauhaus seating. Most of it will be demolished early in the year to make way for a pitch.

Cologne: *RheinheitzgebotStadion*

The eye-catching structure beat Valencia's Androssian Modern Art Gallery and the Rathaus in Copenhagen Zoo as *What New Building?* magazine's Construction of the Year in 2005. Unfortunately, it fell down and has been replaced by something resembling Ashton Gate.

*After publication it was revealed that Pascal Burritzer was not a leading architect, but a crêpe seller in Rouen. Please ignore all information on this page.

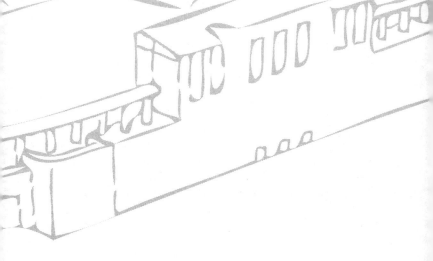

⚽⚽⚽⚽QUIZADINHO

OK, you've heard of Ronaldo and Ronaldinho, but how well do you know the rest of the Brazilian squad? Here are 11 real players and 11 made up ones. Can you pick the team?

Nigelinho ☐

Junior Senior ☐

Dida ☐

Didi ☐

Adriano ☐

Batmani ☐

Robinho ☐

Douwe Egberto ☐

Cafu ☐

Jo ☐

Cappuccino ☐

Fred ☐

Bert ☐

Kaka ☐

Chavalinho ☐

Renato ☐

Renee ☐

Dagoberto ☐

Julio Cesar ☐

Marco Antonio ☐

Vagner Love ☐

Rooninho ☐

True team: Dida, Adriano, Robinho, Cafu, Jo, Fred, Kaka, Renato, Dagoberto, Julio Cesar, Vagner Love
False team: Nigelinho, Junior Senior, Didi, Douwe Egberto, Bert, Cappuccino, Chavalinho, Renee, Marco Antonio, Batmani, Rooninho

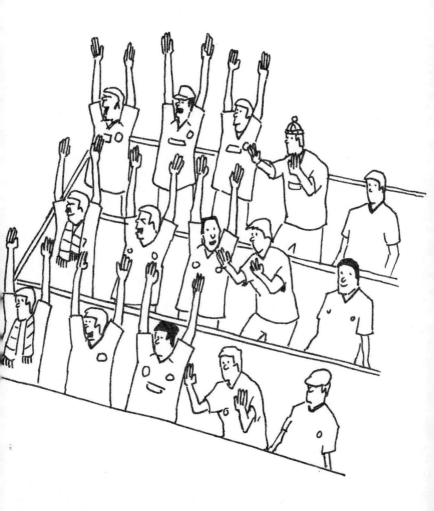

30 pages later, the Mexican wave
was no more interesting.

GERMANY!

⦿⦿⦿⦿COMMENTATOR'S NIGHTMARE XI

1. Abbondanzieri (Argentina)

2. Owomoyela (Germany)

3. Baszczynski (Poland)

4. Yoo Kyoung-ryoul (South Korea)

5. Krstajic (Serbia)

6. Aziawonou (Togo)

7. Srna (Croatia)

8. Gmamdia (Tunisia)

9. Kuijt (Holland)

10. Yanagisawa (Japan)

11. Venhlynskyi (Ukraine)

⚽⚽⚽⚽WHAT'S IN THE STARS FOR THE STARS...

Aquarius – *Roberto Carlos*
You will spend much of the month chasing backwards and forwards.
People speak well of you even if you rarely do anything to merit it. Make
the most of any free-kick within 80 yards of the opponents' goal as this
is your opportunity to belt the ball into row Z and have a little rest from
all that running.

Gemini – *Wayne Rooney*
June should bring lots of opportunity but be careful how you use it.
With *The Sun* right up Uranus for most of the month, I predict masses of
newspaper headlines – until… Oh dear… I see a meeting with a tall man
in black just outside the penalty area.

Scorpio – *Ronaldinho*
You've had a hard season. Your stars say you should rest up a bit this
month – particularly if you are playing an island team from Northern
Europe. Don't try too many of your tricks and try not to humiliate Ashley
Cole. Oh, and by the way, can't you afford to get those teeth done now?

Sagittarius – *Oliver Kahn*
With your moon over the hill, it will be a tough month. Don't be shy of
giving your   e team-mates a rollicking
and remember to bend at the knees when picking the ball out of the net.
You'll meet lots of people in the same profession as you – unfortunately,
none of them will like you.

Virgo – *Hernan Crespo*
If you thought playing (or not playing) at Chelsea this year was
maddening, wait until you meet up with your Argentinian squad. It's
frustrating when no one – apart from you – realizes quite how good you
are. If only you could get to prove it one day. At the end of the month I
see a lot of players in blue waving you off to Italy.

Cancer – *Thierry Henry*
Some things may or may not happen but, of course, it will never be
your fault. There will be a few games when you score lots of goals and
everyone is happy, but come the big match, once again, everyone will be
saying "where's Thierry gone?" You won't mind. Another Renault advert

will come along soon.

Capricorn – *Peter Crouch*

Sometime, towards the end of the month, your moment will have arrived. With just minutes to go, the match in the balance, you replace the crocked Rooney. Beckham plays in the perfect cross... you rise yards above the nearest defender... the ball skims off your head... it sails over the bar and nestles in the lap of a bald man in row Q. England will fly home, you will be sold to a Championship side and eventually open a pub in a south coast holiday town.

Leo – *Francesco Totti*

With Pluto in disgrace this month, Leos will find themselves unsteady on their feet. You may find yourself falling over, even when defenders haven't so much as breathed on you. Come the end of the month, you and your team-mates will feel cheated... still it's better than admitting a better team – like South Korea – beat you.

Pisces – *Jose Antonio Reyes*

I see great hopes for your team and much money being spent at the bookies. Once again, however, there will be much tearing of betting slips. But sometimes life just isn't fair. You seem to be forever dribbling the ball past them, and all the big boys do is kick you. Don't discount the idea of crying for your mummy as you limp off after an ineffectual display against Togo.

Taurus – *Mark Viduka*

OK, you didn't expect to qualify, but now is not the time to be tucking into those bratwurst. Avoid wearing yellow if possible and if you must wear a tracksuit then stay out of sight on the bench – it only upsets people who've paid good money to watch athletes. You'll find those hopeful long balls a little hard to chase so best hang around the penalty box and moan a lot – like usual really.

Aries – *Didier Drogba*

A man with a raised flag will come into your life. Again and again. It might be as well to practice your tantrums, stamping, finger-wagging and cursing now as you might not get many matches to try them out in Germany.

🔵🔵🔵🔵 WHAT'S THE GERMAN FOR...?

If you do happen to be making the trip over to Germany, this selection of phrases might be of some help. The Germans are friendly folk and like to chat about 'fussball' as they call it. And, don't worry, they think Oliver Kahn is an oaf too.

Nice weather for the time of year
Nizzawetter während der Zeit des Jahres

We would like to go to a World Cup football match
Wir möchten gerne ein Weltmeisterschaft Fussballspiel ansehen

---

Please can you direct me to the stadium?
Können bitte Sie direkt ich zum Stadium

Let us hope for a fair game
Lassen Sie uns für ein angemessenes Spiel hoffen

Is that another one of your bent referees?
Ist das eine andere Ihrer Begabungsschiedsrichter?

Oliver Kahn is as mad as a wheelbarrow of fish
Oliver Kahn ist so wütend wie ein Wheelbarrow der Fische

Maybe you just don't have a sense of humour?
Vielleicht haben Sie einfach keinen Sinn für Humor?

Who is the b*****d in the black?
Wer der bastard im Schwarzen ist?

Can you direct me to the nearest knocking shop?
Wo ist die nächste Stadtsbordello bitte?

⦿⦿⦿⦿THE LAUGHTER LINE-UP

It's not big or funny, they're just names... but I dare you not to smile when any of these turn out in Germany...

Goalkeeper:
- Quim (Portugal)

Defenders:
- Lebo Lebo (Angola)
- Eric De Jesus (Ecuador)
- Grosso (Italy)
- Golmohammadi (Iran)

Midfield:
- Yapi (Ivory Coast)
- Vagner Love (Brazil)
- Flavio (Angola)
- Nafti (Tunisia)

Forwards:
- Messi (Argentina)
- Wicky (Switzerland)

Subs:
Nadj (Serbia)
Suziki (Japan)
Scotland (Trinidad & Tobago)
Diana (Italy)
Lee Dong Gook (South Korea)

◎◎◎WORLD CUP PREVIEW

The waiting is over. So how will the 32 teams fare in Germany? This in-depth preview will tell you very little...

GROUP A

Germany
How they qualified: Only just. Even though they get in on the basis of being the host nation, it must have crossed FIFA's mind to 'accidentally' forget about them.

Look out for: Kahn landing one on Lehmann, Ballack vowing never to play again, Klinsmann returning to hiding until the Spurs job comes up and Beckenbauer applying for English nationality.

And... Wouldn't it be great to put them out on penalties – in the semis – in Berlin – and Ballack misses the last.

Costa Rica
How they qualified: Coming third in the North and Central America group they just needed to collect the tops from four cornflake packets to book their place.

Look out for: 72-year-old Paolo Wanchope... he can't still be as crap as he was at Man City 20 years ago, can he?

Poland
How they qualified: Cleaned up on England's sloppy seconds. But boy, are they dull.

Look out for: Absolutely no one. Pick their match for that visit to the wife's mother.

Ecuador
How they qualified: Because they play home games at altitude – 1,850m above sea level – everyone, including Brazil, is knackered after five minutes. All they need is the odd draw in Bolivia or Paraguay and they're in.

Look out for: Former Southampton striker Augustin Delgado, who now plays for Barcelona. OK, the Barcelona that plays in Ecuador.

England

How they qualified: With style, quality football and confidence. OK, it was a bit shaky against Wales, a disaster against Northern Ireland, lucky against Austria and just a relief against Poland. But they made it – somehow.

Look out for: The press hailing them as the greatest team ever after beating the group minnows, followed by a petition to execute Sven when we go out to Brazil on penalties.

Paraguay

How they qualified: Nobody's completely sure they did. Maybe they just turned up at the draw.

Look out for: Their star player, Roque Santa Cruz, who plays for Bayern, knocking Germany out, in Munich.

Trinidad and Tobago

How they qualified: Beat Bahrain in a 'Most Likely Team To Be Patronised' play-off.

Look out for: A balding Dwight Yorke and a host of players from sides in the Conference, Dr Martens Northern Section and the Mrs Briggin's Pies Dorset Sunday League.

Sweden

How they qualified: Although they came second in the group, their goal difference divided by the number of games played, multiplied by 4.3, take away the number you first thought of and… Well they just did, right.

Look out for: An impressive forward line of Ljungberg, Larsson and Ibrahimovic – mind you, the rest of the team is made up of a lot of sturdy blond players who play, have played, or will play for Aston Villa.

GROUP B

Argentina
How they qualified: Strolled in, but still finished second in the South American group to Brazil.

Look out for: Lots of alice bands and sulks. Fabricio Coloccini looks like he's walked straight out of 1970s Led Zeppelin, Sorin really does look like a girl and Tevez is plain ugly.

And… We now know they won't want to meet Michael Owen. They just can't handle the little fella!

Ivory Coast
How they qualified: Beating Cameroon set them up for a clear run.

Look out for: Drogba, Toure and a host of players who'd walk into the England side, being patronised for their 'surprisingly' good performances.

Serbia & Montenegro
How they qualified: Finished ahead of Spain in Group 7. Of course, helped by the fact that they are two countries. Next time maybe we could play as England & Brazil?

Look out for: Mateja Kezman – he may have looked like a waste of space at Chelsea, but here he's an international waste of space.

Holland
How they qualified: With ease. Marco van Basten really has them playing as a team – it won't last.

Look out for: Injury-prone Baldy Robben, misery-prone Ruud van Horse-face and accident-prone van der Sar.

And… The fabulous Oranges breaking into three factions – all of which hate each other and the manager – and going out in a gutless performance against a lowly Scandinavian outfit.

GROUP C

GROUP D

Mexico
How they qualified: Behind the hated USA, but ahead of the drug cartels, puppet states and tin pot juntas that pass as Central America.

Look out for: Bolton striker Javed Borghetti – he may look crap and about 43 years old, but he's Mexico's all-time top scorer.

And... Ageing Mexican hero Hugo Sanchez has such a barney going on with manager Lavolpe, don't put it past him turning up with a sombrero and a Smith & Wesson.

Iran
How they qualified: FIFA – like most of the world – will do anything to piss George Bush off.

Look out for: Their star player, Ali Karimi, who plays for Bayern, knocking Germany out, in Munich.

Angola
How they qualified: Overcame Nigeria (The Black Stars) by having the better nickname. We better watch out. 'The Black Antelopes' sure beats 'Sven's Blue and White Army'.

Look out for: Some brainless commentator calling midfield goalscorer and captain Akwa, the 'new' Davids, Essien, Gullit...

Portugal
How they qualified: Waltzed through the group. Talented, confident, stylish... what could go wrong? Everything. It's Portugal...

Look out for: Big Phil Scolari's under-arm sweat patches growing with each game.

And... Figo standing with hands on hips like he's had enough, Cristiano Ronaldo crying and Deco wishing he'd played for Brazil after all.

GROUP E

Italy

How they qualified: Impressively for a change – apart from an embarrassing defeat to Slovenia.

Look out for: Gattuso kicking anything that moves, Totti falling over every time the ball is remotely near him and Del Piero going missing like a wartime sub.

And... Blaming anything or anybody but themselves and their own incompetence for their exit.

Ghana

How they qualified: Somehow managed to finish ahead of the mighty Democratic Republic of Congo and the perennially over-rated South Africa.

Look out for: Michael Essien. Will he look quite so good without Frank Lampard by his side? Quite possibly he'll be better.

USA

How they qualified: Mistakenly entered the World Cup thinking that, like their 'World Series', the 'World' constituted the mid-west, California and Toronto.

Look out for: Their massive away following – five High School geography teachers from Minnesota.

And... Hope for a game against Mexico – they really do hate each other.

Czech Republic

How they qualified: Did for the Norwegians in a play-off!

Look out for: The rare sight of Petr Cech picking the ball from his net.

And... Lank-haired prima dona Pavel Nedved, who at the ripe old age of 29, couldn't possibly lift his weary limbs for his country until generously coming out of retirement for the play-offs. I bet he fancies it now though.

Brazil
How they qualified: Beat everyone...blah blah... Beautiful football... blah blah... Best in the World... Oh, they lost to Ecuador!

Look out for: The Famous Five – Ronaldinho, Ronaldo, Robinho, Adriano and Timmy the Dog.

And... Where do they get those good-looking women supporters? England only ever get sad, 14 stone, menopausal women with woolly scarves covered in badges and a hot dog in each hand.

Croatia
How they qualified: They won Group 8 ahead of Sweden and Bulgaria. No, that doesn't tell us much.

Look out for: Their best player, Glasgow Rangers' Prso, who scores for pleasure in Scotland – mind you, so does John Hartson.

And... Let's hope for a match against Serbia and Montenegro. It could make England v Argentina look like a tea party.

Australia
How they qualified: After a tough qualifying group, including the Soloman Islands and the Captain Bligh Islands, the Aussies squeezed into the finals on penalties against Uruguay. Scary? I don't think so.

Look out for: Lard-arse Viduka and Harry Kewell (if he can be bothered to get on the plane) will be good for a laugh.

And... The Socceroos (can anyone take a team called 'the Socceroos' seriously?) might get good support in Germany, but it'll be a bugger trying to get served in any London pub.

Japan
How they qualified: Threatened to ruin the German car industry if they weren't invited.

Look out for: Yuji Nakazawa, candidate for most ridiculous hairstyle – think of a cross between David Cassidy and Jesus.

GROUP F

France

How they qualified: Desperately. When all looked lost, a begging letter from manager Domenech brought back Zidane, who also got his mates Makelele and Thuram out of bed.

Look out for: Don't expect the French nation to rise as one to salute the efforts of Les Bleus. When they're not setting fire to cars, tossing frozen sheep and claiming EU subsidies, they are still more interested in debating the absurdity of existence than football.

Switzerland

How they qualified: Legging it down the tunnel away from coaching staff, soldiers, kebab sellers and 110,000 fuming Turks.

Look out for: As 'neutrals', the Swiss are not allowed to beat or lose to anyone, so they might only collect three points. Of course, they are really on the Germans' side.

South Korea

How they qualified: Through the Asian rounds – although everyone wanted them back so they can humiliate Italy again.

Look out for: Wenger and Ferguson desperately scanning the squad for someone to sit on their bench and sell lots of shirts in the Far East.

Togo

How they qualified: Every World Cup, FIFA picks a team that no one has ever heard of. Wales just missed out again.

Look out for: Commentators going on about witch doctors… again.

And… Apparently, the USA team think they are a pizza delivery company.

GROUP G

GROUP H

Spain
How they qualified: Think they are something for tearing Slovakia apart. Of course, if they were that good, they wouldn't have even been in the play-offs.

Look out for: All the experts tipping Raul, Torres and Co for big success again. There are only two certainties in every World Cup: Pele picks some no-mark (yes, you, Nicky Butt) as the greatest player in the world and the Spanish disappoint again.

Ukraine
How they qualified: Survivors of the Group of Death ahead of Denmark, Greece and Turkey.

Look out for: Andrii Shevchenko, the goal-machine that Roman Abramovic is having to save up for.

Tunisia
How they qualified: Kings of the Desert, having defeated their great rivals Morocco.

Look out for: Their Brazilian born star, Francileudo dos Santos, or 'the big fella' as Jack Charlton will, no doubt, call him.

Saudi Arabia
How they qualified: Masterful completion, in under nine words, of FIFA's competition, "We would like to play in the World Cup because..."

Look out for: A monumental thrashing from a team who themselves are not too good.

WHAT THEY SAY...

A spot of handbags...
He'll be disappointed with that...
A pocket battleship...
A volatile player...

He's got a bag of tricks...

He's a good shot-stopper...
Full blooded-tackle...
Plucky Africans/Asians/Antipodeans etc...
There are no minnows...
These two teams are cancelling each other out...
Box-to-box player...
Unhappy with that decision...

Breaking up play...

Free-kick expert...
Some naïve defending...
A little loose at the back...
A classic South American player...
I'm not sure there was contact...
That's a touching goal celebration...
I think it could be a hamstring problem...
The ref's up with play...
Pulled off at half-time...

Aggressive play...
Not a classic so far...
A wholehearted player...

...WHAT THEY MEAN☺☺☺☺☺☺☺☺☺☺☺☺☺☺☺☺☺☺☺☺☺☺

... It's not like my day when men were men.

... How much does he get paid?

... He's under five foot eleven and kicks people.

... Takes every refereeing decision as a personal affront and would probably be in prison if he didn't play football.

... He does a step-over, three lollipops, a Cruyff turn and then crosses into the back of the stand.

... He can't catch crosses.

... Tried to take his opponent's leg off.

... We just got outclassed by players I've never heard of.

... Please don't let us lose to this bunch of no-hopers.

... What's on the other channel?

... Runs about a lot to little effect.

... He's used the f-word eight times in a sentence and is throttling the ref.

... He's fallen over again and is writhing around like he's been bitten in the balls by a pit-bull.

... Once got lucky but yet again is sending this one out of the ground.

... An African side has let in a goal.

... A European side has let in a goal.

... A cheat.

... The German is diving again.

...Oh no! They're doing that dreadful baby rocking again.

... Do I look like a doctor?

... This makes the ref's decision even worse

... He's been substituted, unless of course it's Sven they're talking about in which case it could be anything.

... Cover your children's eyes, there's going to be blood.

... Try not to fall asleep on the sofa.

... How did he make it to the World Cup Finals?

GLOSSARY

4–4–2 Winning team formation, unless Brazil play something else.

4–3–3 The Dambusters squadron number.

2–1–1–2–3–5 Silly formation, possibly used by ladies' hockey teams.

The Beautiful Game Monopoly.

Booking The ref's taken a fancy to you and has taken your name.

Cattenacio Like fellatio but with cats.

Coach/Head coach/Selector/Team guru
Foreign-talk for manager, usually has bushy moustache, sweat patches and smokes fags.

Counter-attacking game Hoofing it upfield to a hulking oaf of a centre-forward.

Cultured left-foot Goes to the opera, while the right one lies on the couch watching *Hollyoaks*.

Double-booking The ref doesn't like you any more and you're off his Christmas list as well as the pitch.

Early Doors Jim Morrison's 'Light My Fire' period.

England's left-sided problem Owen Hargreaves.

Flat back four IKEA defensive kit.

Golden Boot The latest over-priced trainers.

Good Engine Traded in his BMW for a Jeep.

Group of death Usually Group E, where the losers are sent to a military dictatorship and are summarily executed.

Holding player A defender, called a midfielder, but who plays in defence.

Long ball game Hoofing it upfield to a hulking oaf of a centre-forward.

Magic Sponge
A sponge… that's magic. It's used to cure all ailments that footballers could ever possibly suffer from.

Offside If, when the ball is kicked and unless he's not interfering… He just is. OK!

Offside trap Underhand scheme operated by match-strangling foreigners or masterly precise defending by our brave lads.

Penalty Where a bloke who is paid £80,000 a week worries about hitting a huge box from 12 yards.

Playing in the hole Abuse aimed at forward who can't be bothered to join the attack.

Round of 16 What the bloke in front of you at the bar is buying as England's penalty shoot-out begins.

Playmaker Bloke with a ponytail, poncing about in midfield.

Stoppage time
Tedious match-ending where bonehead forward repeatedly dribbles to corner flag where six defenders take it in turns to try and break his ankle.

WHO DO YOU
THINK YOU
ARE KIDDING
MR. KLINSMANN?

A Wasteful World Cup banner, colour it in and wave it at the Germans on tv – or at the match if you are lucky enough to attend one.